D1335726

FIREFIGHTING

The Financial Crisis and Its Lessons

BEN S. BERNANKE,
TIMOTHY F. GEITHNER,
AND HENRY M. PAULSON, JR.

P

PROFILE BOOKS

First published in Great Britain in 2019 by
Profile Books Ltd
3 Holford Yard
Bevin Way
London
WC1X 9HD

www.profilebooks.com

First published in the United States of America in 2019 by
Penguin Books, an imprint of Penguin Random House LLC

Copyright © Ben S. Benanke, Timothy F. Geithner and Henry M. Paulson, Jr, 2019

1 3 5 7 9 10 8 6 4 2

Printed and bound by
CPI Group (UK) Ltd, Croydon, CR0 4YY

A CIP catalogue record for this book is available from the British Library.

ISBN 978 1 78816 336 1
eISBN 978 1 78283 605 6

FSC
www.fsc.org
MIX
Paper from
responsible sources
FSC® C018072

We dedicate this book to the many public servants—of both parties and in both the legislative and executive branches— who worked closely with us in the fight against the global financial crisis. Special thanks are due to Presidents George W. Bush and Barack Obama for their leadership and to the staffs of the Federal Reserve, Treasury, the FDIC, and other agencies for their creativity and hard work in the service of our country.

Contents

FIREFIGHTING

INTRODUCTION

EPIC FINANCIAL INFERNOS DON'T HAPPEN OFTEN. USUALLY, turmoil in financial markets burns itself out. Markets adjust, firms fail, and life goes on. Sometimes, financial fires get so serious that policymakers need to help put them out. They make loans when firms need liquidity, or find a safe way to wind down a troubled firm, and life goes on. It's exceedingly rare that a fire rages out of control, threatening to consume the financial system and the rest of the economy, creating extreme disruption and deprivation. It happened in the United States during the Great Depression, and then it didn't happen again for seventy-five years.

But it happened again in 2008. The United States government—two successive presidents, Congress, the Federal Reserve, the Treasury Department, and thousands of public servants at a variety of agencies—had to confront the worst financial crisis in generations. And the three of us were in positions of responsibility—Ben S. Bernanke as chairman of the Federal Reserve; Henry M. Paulson, Jr., as secretary of the Treasury under President George W. Bush; Timothy F. Geithner as president of the Federal Reserve Bank of New York during the Bush years and then Treasury secretary under President Barack Obama. We helped shape the American and international response to a conflagration that choked off global credit, ravaged global finance, and plunged the

American economy into the most damaging recession since the breadlines and shantytowns of the 1930s.

Along with our colleagues at the Fed, Treasury, and other agencies, we fought the fire with an extraordinary barrage of emergency interventions, escalating from conventional and then unconventional loans to government rescues of major firms and government backstops for vital credit markets. When the fire kept raging, we persuaded Congress to give us even more powerful tools to fight it, including the authority to inject hundreds of billions of dollars of capital directly into private financial institutions. Working alongside an outstanding group of dedicated public officials in the United States and around the world, we eventually helped stabilize the financial system before frozen credit channels and collapsing asset values could drag the broader economy into a second Depression. Even so, the economy suffered a major downturn, and unprecedented monetary and fiscal stimulus would be needed to help jump-start the recovery.

This was a classic financial panic, reminiscent of runs and crises that have afflicted finance for hundreds of years. We know from that long experience that the damage inflicted by financial panics is never limited to the financial sector, even though the strategies for stopping them require support for the financial sector. Americans who aren't bankers or investors still rely on a functioning credit system to buy cars and homes, borrow for college, and grow their businesses. Financial crises that damage the credit system can create brutal recessions that hurt ordinary families as well as financial elites. Today, much of the American public remembers the government's interventions as a bailout for Wall Street, but our goal was always to protect Main Street from the fallout of a financial collapse. The only way to contain the economic damage of a financial fire is to put it out, even though it's almost impossible to do that without helping some of the people who caused it.

Ten years later, we thought it would be useful to look back at how the crisis unfolded, and to consider the lessons that might help reduce the damage from future crises. All three of us have already written memoirs about our experiences, but we wanted to speak about what we did together and what we learned together, about the theory and practice of financial firefighting. We have very different backgrounds and very different personalities. We did not know one another well before the crisis. But we found ways to collaborate effectively as we worked to put out the fire, and we agree that some basic principles could apply to fighting any fire in the financial sector. Financial crises recur in part because memories fade. We're writing about this again to help convey some of the key lessons from our experience, in the hope that it will keep memories fresh and help firefighters of the future protect economies from the ravages of financial crises.

Why did this crisis happen, and why was it so damaging?

It was, again, a classic financial panic, a run on the financial system triggered by a crisis of confidence in mortgages. It was fueled, as crises usually are, by a credit boom, in which many families as well as financial institutions became dangerously overleveraged, financing themselves almost entirely with debt. The danger was heightened because so much risk had migrated to financial institutions that operated outside the constraints and protections of the traditional banking system, and because so much of the leverage was in the form of unstable short-term financing that could vanish at the first hint of trouble. These vulnerabilities were allowed to fester by America's balkanized financial regulatory bureaucracy, a hodgepodge of agencies and authorities and regulations that for decades had failed to keep pace with changing market realities and rapid financial innovations. And one of those innovations, securitization, the mechanism Wall Street used to slice and dice mortgages into complex financial products that became ubiquitous in modern finance, helped transform panic about the risks embedded in underlying mortgages into panic about the stability of the entire system.

These problems did not seem pressing during the boom, when the financial system appeared unusually stable, conventional wisdom held that home prices would continue to rise indefinitely, and many in Wall Street, Washington, and academia believed that serious financial crises were a thing of the past. But once the housing bubble popped, fear of losses created a financial stampede, as investors and creditors frantically reduced their exposure to anything and anyone associated with mortgage-backed securities, triggering fire sales (where cash-starved investors are forced to sell their assets at any price) and margin calls (where investors who bought assets on credit are forced to put up more cash) that in turn triggered more fire sales and margin calls. The financial panic paralyzed credit and shattered confidence in the broader economy, and the resulting job losses and foreclosures in turn created more panic in the financial system.

A decade later, that doom loop of financial fear and economic pain has begun to recede in the public memory. But it's hard to overstate just how chaotic and frightening it was. A one-month period starting in September 2008 included the sudden nationalization of the mortgage giants Fannie Mae and Freddie Mac, the largest and most surprising government intervention in financial markets since the Depression; the failure of the venerable investment bank Lehman Brothers, the largest bankruptcy in U.S. history; the collapse of the brokerage firm Merrill Lynch into the arms of Bank of America; an $85 billion government rescue of the insurer AIG to prevent an even larger bankruptcy than Lehman's; the two largest failures of federally insured banks in U.S. history, those of Washington Mutual and Wachovia; the extinction of the investment bank model that had become synonymous with modern Wall Street; the first-ever government guarantees for more than $3 trillion worth of money market funds; the backstopping of a further $1 trillion worth of commercial paper; and congressional approval, after an initial market-crushing rejection, of a $700 billion arsenal of government support for the entire financial system. This all happened during the stretch run of a presidential campaign. Vladimir Lenin supposedly said that there are some decades when nothing happens, and some weeks when decades happen—that's what it felt like in the crisis.

The powers of the government's crisis managers initially proved insufficient to stop the panic, in part because so many of the problems began outside the Fed's principal jurisdiction of commercial banks. But we eventually persuaded Congress to give us the authority we needed to restore confidence in the system, and the stampeders eventually did stop stampeding. At a time of intense partisanship and pervasive skepticism about government, a Republican and then a Democratic administration worked together with nonpartisan public servants and (at times) bipartisan legislative leaders to defuse the most serious threat to capitalism in generations.

We are all believers in the power of free markets, and we were all reluctant to rescue reckless bankers and investors from their own mistakes. When possible, the U.S. government imposed tough terms on firms receiving aid; sometimes, the imperative to persuade stronger institutions as well as weaker ones to participate in efforts to strengthen the system and revive confidence limited how tough the terms of the programs could be. But we knew that stepping back and letting nature take its course was not a reasonable choice. The invisible hand of capitalism can't stop a full-blown financial collapse; only the visible hand of government can do that. And full-blown financial collapses create vicious recessions that kill businesses, limit opportunities, and frustrate dreams.

In fact, the financial shocks of 2008 were by many measures greater than the shocks before the Great Depression, and so was the initial economic impact. By year's end, even after a remarkably aggressive series of financial interventions, the U.S. economy was hemorrhaging 750,000 jobs a month and shrinking at a depression-level 8 percent annual rate. But the economic contraction popularly known as the Great Recession was over by June 2009, and the ensuing recovery is now ten years old and counting—an impressive turnaround compared with previous crises or other developed nations after this crisis. The U.S. stock market, labor market, and housing market have all rebounded from their depths and ascended to new heights. Experts predicted that the strategy we adopted would end in hyperinflation, economic stagnation, and fiscal ruin, and that the government's efforts to rescue floundering banks and ultimately the entire financial system would cost taxpayers trillions of dollars without fixing the underlying problems. But we were able to get the economy growing and the financial sector working again relatively quickly, and the various financial programs ended up turning a sizable profit for the U.S. taxpayer. The crisis was devastating, inflicting deep and lasting scars on individual families, the broader economy, and the American political system. But the damage would have been far worse without the concerted and powerful rescue efforts that the United States was ultimately able to mobilize.

Are we safer now?

The United States and the world have enacted sweeping financial reforms, which should reduce the probability of another disaster in the near future. In part because of these reforms, financial institutions have more capital, less leverage, more liquidity, and less dependence on tenuous short-term financing. In short, our financial fire codes are stronger today. Unfortunately, prevention is never foolproof, just as no building is ever fireproof. And especially in the United States, where government interventions provoked such a strong public backlash, politicians have weakened the fire department's ability to respond to the next crisis, taking important powers away from crisis managers in the hope of avoiding future bailouts. In reality, those limitations, however well intentioned, are likely to make the next crisis worse, and the resulting economic damage more severe. The belief that legislation that purports to ban bailouts will actually prevent them in all future scenarios is a powerful but dangerous illusion.

The backlash was inevitable, and understandable. The government's actions to stop the panic and fix the broken financial system, although ultimately successful, did not protect millions of people from the loss of a job or a home. They did, unavoidably, benefit many individuals who had participated in that broken system, and some who had helped set it ablaze. Still, the next time a financial fire breaks out, America may well wish it had a better-prepared firehouse with better-equipped firefighters. One reason the crisis was so damaging was that the government lacked the tools needed to attack it with overwhelming force from the start. We fear that unless Washington makes significant changes, the first responders of the future will start with even fewer and even weaker tools—and just as we did, they'll have to lobby politicians to upgrade the fire department while the fire is already burning.

We want America to be ready for the fire next time, to borrow a phrase from James Baldwin, because eventually the fire will come. That's why we think it's so important to try to understand the last crisis—how it started, how it spread, why it burned so hot, how we and our colleagues struggled to fight it, what worked, and what didn't. We're afraid a nation that doesn't understand the lessons of this meltdown might be doomed to endure something even worse.

Some of those lessons are about prediction and prevention, because the best way to minimize the damage from a financial crisis is not to have one. Most crises do follow a similar pattern, so it's possible to try to identify warning signs, like excessive leverage in the financial system, especially when it's too dependent on short-term financing, particularly in corners of the system with weak fire codes and limited access to the firehouse. But it's also important to have humility about the ability of human beings to anticipate panics, because doing so requires them to anticipate the behavior of other human beings interacting in complex systems. Financial systems are inherently fragile, and financial risk tends to migrate around regulatory obstacles, like a river flowing around rocks. There's no sure way to avoid a panic, because there's no sure way to avoid overconfidence or confusion. Human beings are human, which is why we think it makes sense to think about crises the way Buddhists think about death: with uncertainty about the timing and circumstances, but certainty that it will happen eventually.

The crisis also gave us a lot of experience in the art and science of crisis response. As hard as it is to predict crises in advance, it's also hard to know early in a crisis whether it's just a brush fire or the start of a five-alarm conflagration. It's usually healthy to allow failing firms to fail, and policymakers shouldn't overreact to every air pocket in the market or setback for a big bank as if it's the precursor to a catastrophe. Responding too quickly can encourage risk takers to believe they'll never face consequences for their bad bets, creating "moral hazard" that can promote even more irresponsible speculation and set the stage for future crises. But once it's clear that a crisis is truly systemic, underreacting is much more dangerous than overreacting, too late creates more problems than too early, and half measures can just pour gasoline on the flames. The top priority in an epic crisis should always be to end it, even though that will likely create some moral hazard; the downsides of encouraging undisciplined risk taking in the future, while real, pale in comparison to the downsides of allowing a systemic collapse in the present. When panic strikes, policymakers need to do everything in their power to quell it, regardless of the political ramifications, regardless of their ideological convictions, regardless of what they've said or promised in the past. The politics of financial rescues are terrible, but economic depressions are worse.

We have no easy solutions for improving the politics of crisis response, but we do hope that we can help provide some context for the choices we made and update the playbook for first responders in future crises. We'll try to address some of the lingering questions about our decisions, such as why the government couldn't rescue Lehman Brothers when it did rescue AIG, and why we didn't try to break up the Wall Street megabanks after the crisis ended. We'll also discuss some other lessons of the crisis, including the importance of pairing efforts to stabilize the financial system with stimulus programs that stabilize the broader economy, and the need for government regulation of financial firms that aren't traditional commercial banks but can pose similar risks to the system. We'll talk about the challenges of decision making in the fog of a financial war, and about how important it is to have teams of experienced and dedicated professionals in the Treasury, the Fed, the Federal Deposit Insurance Corporation, and other agencies who are willing to work cooperatively rather than competitively. We'll discuss the power and the limits of the post-crisis reforms, and how we believe they could be improved. And even though none of us is a politician, we have some things to say about the political process, which we often found depressing and frustrating, but sometimes quite inspiring.

The tone for the political process is set at the top. At an extraordinarily dangerous moment in our history, Presidents Bush and Obama both had the political courage to support tremendously unpopular but critical interventions in the financial system. And while we had our share of complaints about Congress, Republican and Democratic legislative leaders came together when it counted to back the politically toxic efforts to nationalize Fannie Mae and Freddie Mac and then rescue the entire financial system, which turned out to be the last two major pieces of American legislation to pass with significant bipartisan support. The 2008 crisis and the painful recession that followed heavily damaged trust in public institutions, but we believe America's response to the crisis demonstrated what's possible when public officials at all levels of government work together under intense stress for the public good.

We understand why many Americans don't see the government's response to the crisis as successful or even legitimate. It looked messy and inconsistent, because it often was; we were feeling our way in the dark, trying to navigate the here-be-dragons section of the financial map. We initially followed a traditional playbook, but the modern financial system is far more complex than it used to be, so we had to do a lot of experimentation and escalation. We struggled to fight the fire with tools we didn't consider sufficient for the job, and then we struggled to persuade politicians to give us more powerful tools. And while there were no magic words we could have said to persuade the public to embrace bank bailouts or other controversial policies, we constantly struggled to communicate what we were doing and why.

We hope we can do a better job of that now. The story of the crisis is a painful story, but it is in some ways a hopeful story. We believe it can also be a helpful story.

CHAPTER ONE

DRY TINDER:
The Roots of the Crisis

THE SPARK FOR THE FINANCIAL FIRE OF 2008 CAME FROM IR- responsible lending in America's subprime mortgage sector. But the turmoil in that chaotic though relatively small corner of the credit markets could not have created a global inferno if dry tinder hadn't accumulated throughout the entire financial system. The subprime meltdown was the immediate cause of the crisis, but there were deeper underlying causes that made a fragile system vulnerable to disaster. To understand the roots of the crisis, it's important to know why the spark ignited, but also to know what made the forest so flammable. And understanding the roots of this crisis is important to understanding how to reduce the likelihood and intensity of future crises.

History doesn't repeat itself, but as Mark Twain supposedly said, it often rhymes. This crisis followed the pattern of epic crises of the past—mania followed by panic followed by crash, in the formulation of the economic historian Charles Kindleberger—with modern twists that made the panic even more difficult to anticipate and contain. It began, like every major crisis, with a borrowing frenzy, a credit boom during a time of overconfidence that went bust when the confidence disappeared. And the financial system reflected the overconfidence of the boom. Financial firms took on too much risky leverage. Much of that leverage was in the form of "runnable" short-term debt that could disappear whenever creditors got jittery. Much of the risk migrated to firms outside the traditional banking system, where regulation and supervisory oversight were inadequate and the safety net designed to protect banks in an emergency was inaccessible. And a wide range of financial institutions were too exposed to mortgages through direct and indirect channels, including the ubiquitous mortgage-backed securities that were considered safe during the housing bubble but became toxic once the bubble popped. That helped spread investor panic, from securities backed by shoddy subprime mortgages to all mortgage securities, and then to firms believed to be exposed to those securities, and even to firms believed to be exposed to other firms exposed to those securities. Panic is contagious.

These problems can seem obvious with the benefit of a decade of hindsight, but they were not widely understood at the time. While all crises begin with credit booms, not all credit booms end in crises, and the financial system seemed more stable than ever in the early years of the twenty-first century; 2005 was the first year without a U.S. bank failure since the Depression. The boom was masking some serious long-term economic challenges for America—rising income inequality, persistently stagnant wages, slow productivity growth, a troubling decline in labor participation for working-age men—but overall the U.S. economy seemed in pretty good shape. There was also widespread confidence that if the economy did stumble, the financial system would be resilient. It had, after all, weathered a series of modest recessions and other tests reasonably well in the previous decades, and banks seemed to have plenty of capital to absorb losses in case of a downturn. At the time, serious economists were arguing that financial innovations like derivatives, because of their purported ability to better diversify risks, had made crises a thing of the past.

But financial crises will never be a thing of the past. Long periods of stability can create overconfidence that breeds instability, as the economist Hyman Minsky famously observed. It is during those boom times, when liquidity seems limitless and asset values seem destined to keep rising, that risk taking tends to get excessive, posing dangers that can extend well beyond the risk takers.

Before the crisis, none of us fully appreciated the vulnerabilities that were building in our financial system. But none of us ever believed financial crises were obsolete, perhaps because we had spent so much of our careers thinking about them—Ben in academia, Tim in government, and Hank in markets. As a Princeton University economics professor, Ben had been a scholar of the Great Depression, the leading historical example of financial instability sinking the economy. As a career public servant at Treasury and later the International Monetary Fund, Tim had seen the challenges in dealing with financial crises in Mexico, Asia, and around the world. And as the CEO of Goldman Sachs, Hank had lived through episodes like the collapse of the hedge fund Long-Term Capital Management and the Russian default. We had all learned how quickly overheated markets could collapse, and while none of us was as worried as we should have been, none of us thought that financial innovations and the sophistication of modern finance had immunized us against crisis.

The financial system is vital to the economy. But finance, at least as it's organized in modern economies, is inherently fragile. Before we discuss the specific factors that made the system unusually vulnerable to panic a decade ago, it's worth touching on why the system is, was, and always will be vulnerable to panic.

THE CONFIDENCE GAME

The basic vulnerability of the financial system stems from the fact that banks provide two important economic functions that occasionally come into conflict. They give people an easily accessible place to stash their money that provides more safety and a higher interest rate than a mattress; then they provide loans with that money to finance riskier investments in homes, cars, and businesses that improve living standards and make economies go. In other words, they borrow short-term in order to lend long-term, a process known as "maturity transformation." This can be an efficient way to allocate capital to productive uses, giving society as a whole the ability to commit resources to long-lived, illiquid investments that create prosperity and progress while still giving individual members of society access to their cash when they need it.

But maturity transformation comes with some risks. Every institution that borrows short and lends long is vulnerable to a "run on the bank," as in the famous scene at Bailey Bros. Building & Loan Association in *It's a Wonderful Life*. As Jimmy Stewart's George Bailey had to explain to the residents of Bedford Falls who were clamoring for their money, very little of the cash that depositors and other short-term creditors lend to a bank is actually kept in the bank. This can be a problem in those rare situations where creditors lose confidence in the bank and demand their money back at the same time. And in those rare situations, it's a serious problem, because most of their money has already been lent out. Even a solvent bank, with assets more valuable than its liabilities, can collapse if those assets are too illiquid to cover its creditors' immediate demands for cash.

The United States, like most countries, has tried to reduce this risk with regulations that limit the risks banks are allowed to take, coupled with government-provided insurance for depositors that reduces their incentive to run if their bank seems unstable. But most banks that accept deposits still depend on other forms of funding that remain uninsured and runnable. And in the modern age, a run on a bank no longer requires a physical run to an actual bank, just a click of a mouse. This makes banks and other financial intermediaries particularly sensitive to outbreaks of fear. Prudential regulations can constrain this risk but cannot eliminate it, not as long as banks are in the business of maturity transformation and making inherently risky loans to individuals and businesses.

The more general point is that financial institutions, unlike other businesses whose success depends primarily on the cost and quality of their goods and services, are dependent on confidence. That's why the word "credit" comes from the Latin for "belief," why we say we can "bank" on things we know to be true, why some financial institutions are called "trusts." It's why traditional bank architecture relied so heavily on imposing granite facades and pillars to project an aura of stability and permanence in front of the fragility of finance. No financial institution can function without confidence, and confidence is evanescent. It can go at any time, for rational or irrational reasons. When it goes, it usually goes quickly, and it's hard to get back.

A financial crisis is a bank run writ large, a crisis of confidence throughout the system. People get scared and want their money back, which makes the money remaining in the system less safe, which makes more people want their money back, a self-reinforcing doom loop of fear, fire sales, capital shortfalls, margin calls, and credit contractions that can produce a stampede for the exits. Once a stampede begins, it becomes rational to run to avoid getting trampled, and hesitation can be deadly. Perception and reality both matter, because runners will keep running until they're confident not only that they don't have a rational reason to run, but that others will have the confidence to stop running as well. Fear is hardwired into the human psyche, and the herd mentality is powerful, which makes stampedes hard to predict and hard to stop. The potential for panic can never be fully eradicated.

In other words, the world will face the threat of financial crises as long as risk taking and maturity transformation remain central to finance, and as long as humans remain human. Unfortunately, disaster will always be possible.

So what made this particular disaster happen?

THE SOURCE OF THE SPARK

The years before the crisis saw a rapid buildup of debt in the United States. Ordinary families got dangerously overextended. The ratio of household debt to GDP rose so rapidly that Tim started calling the chart he used to track it "Mount Fuji." Commercial banks, investment banks, insurance companies, mortgage companies, finance companies, pension funds, and mutual funds from the United States and around the world provided this credit; what's more, they often borrowed to provide that credit, accumulating $36 trillion worth of leveraged assets financed with fragile funding. As a nation, America was living beyond its means—and living off the savings of other countries. A tidal wave of foreign money was pouring into the United States, as global investors frustrated by low interest rates and scarce investment opportunities at home looked abroad for better and safer yields. Ben called this seemingly insatiable demand for assets that generated decent returns a "global savings glut," and it created a lot of dry tinder.

The greatest part of the credit boom took place in the U.S. mortgage market. Mortgage debt per U.S. household soared 63 percent from 2001 to 2007, much faster than household incomes. Some of this new debt was beneficial, helping people buy homes or take cash out of their homes for worthy purposes. But some of the new lending veered into dangerous, unexplored territory, where the underwriting standards, especially for higher-risk sub-prime mortgages to lower-income borrowers, eroded dramatically. Many lenders would approve almost any applicant to borrow just about the entire cost of a new home regardless of their credit history—whether or not they had a job, provided any documents verifying their income, or demonstrated any realistic hope of making their monthly payments. There were "NINJA" loans for borrowers with no proof of income, job, or assets; "liar loans" to folks who inflated their annual salaries or lied about their assets; "exploding ARMs" with teaser rates that skyrocketed after two or three years—anything to get a signature on the dotted line.

Normally, lenders have strong incentives to be careful about how much they lend and to whom, because they need to get paid back to make money. But in the years before the crisis, Wall Street firms responded to the ferocious global appetite for safe-looking assets by packaging mortgages into increasingly elaborate mortgage-backed securities that they could sell to investors looking for higher returns. This investor demand gave those Wall Street firms an equally ferocious appetite for mortgages that could serve as the raw materials for these securities. And loan originators who knew they could sell their mortgages without retaining any of the risk of default had little incentive to seek creditworthy borrowers. Many of them even received bonuses determined by the volume of loans generated rather than their quality. These loans became grist for a lucrative mill that divided the payment streams from mortgages with different degrees of risk and then repackaged them into complex securities, until the risk was sliced so fine it seemed to disappear. Of course, it did not disappear. It was just hidden and diluted and spread around the world.

The "originate-to-distribute" mortgage model created bad incentives for mortgage originators, and some analysts have blamed it for the entire crisis. In this view, disaster could have been averted if lenders had been required to hold more of the loans they originated, because they wouldn't have been so reckless if they had more skin in the game. But the undeniable problems with that model can't tell the whole story, as many of those lenders and their parent companies did hold many of their loans, as well as securities backed by their loans, and accepted them as solid collateral in short-term lending markets. Firms like Countrywide Financial, the nation's largest and most aggressive mortgage lender, had plenty of skin in the game; they stumbled because they didn't distribute *enough* of the risky loans they originated. They were like drug dealers who got high on their own supply, genuinely believing that stratospheric housing prices would defy gravity indefinitely.

Ultimately, the basic driver of the boom in mortgage borrowing was excessive optimism about the housing market. Rising house prices promoted easy borrowing terms, and easy terms in turn helped drive prices even higher. There was a widespread assumption that borrowers could buy more house than they could afford without significant risk, because if they had trouble making the payments they could always refinance or sell at a profit—and for years that rosy assumption was often correct. One 2014 study published in the *American Economic Review* found that even mortgage brokers and Wall Street bankers invested their own money in real estate throughout the boom. They were just as caught up in the mania as the buyers of their mortgage-backed securities. The executives of the venerable 150-year-old investment bank Lehman Brothers were similarly deluded, concluding a wildly misguided $22 billion purchase of the massive real estate firm Archstone-Smith Trust after the bust had already begun. The mania ran broad and deep.

In any event, the poor quality of many newly issued mortgages would have a major impact on the stability of the financial system. The direct losses on mortgages would have been a problem in itself, though probably a manageable one. But the securitization boom carved those mortgages into securities that became a common form of currency and collateral throughout the financial system. These securities often received triple-A stamps of approval from credit ratings agencies that depended on the issuers of the securities for their fees, and markets often treated them as if they were almost as safe as Treasuries. The flawed models justifying those triple-A ratings depended in part on the belief that even if housing prices did slump in one region of the country, they would never crash all across the country at the same time. That had been true since World War II, partly as a result of tax policies and government programs designed to promote and expand home ownership. But the optimistic assumption that securities assembled from geographically diverse mortgages would continue to avoid the risk of mass defaults turned out to be wrong. Ultimately, home prices plunged more than 30 percent nationwide, and the percentage of subprime mortgages in or near default soared from 6 percent to more than 30 percent. The carnage was worst in "sand states" like Florida and Nevada, where the run-up in prices had been the greatest, but it was bad almost everywhere.

Again, the systemic danger was not just that mortgages were less safe than they seemed. The systemic danger was that the securities they backed had come to underpin much of modern finance, which made the health of the entire financial system dependent on the perceived condition of the mortgage market in ways few people recognized at the time. That dependence would have been dangerous even if the securities had been straightforward, transparent, and traded on public exchanges. But "collateralized debt obligations," "CDOs-Squared," and other new products of financial engineering were often complex, opaque, and embedded with hidden leverage. These products were supposed to help reduce risk by spreading it around and customizing it to the needs of the investor, but, in the confluence of forces at the end of the long boom in credit, they made the overall system both more vulnerable to a crisis of confidence and harder to stabilize after the crisis began. Once mortgages started to go bad and the complex securities constructed from mortgages started to seem risky, it felt easier and safer to sell them en masse than to try to figure out just how risky individual securities were. Meanwhile, the market for buying and selling derivatives—financial assets whose values were tied in complicated ways to the values of other assets—was an archaic mess of millions of contracts among thousands of private counterparties, where at times it seemed nearly impossible to figure out who held what and who owed what to whom. That meant that in a crisis, investors and creditors would be uncertain what exposures they had or what was going on with their counterparties. And uncertainty is like gasoline on the fire of panic.

Still, at the time, the subprime mortgage market did not look like a threat to burn down the financial system. Subprime mortgages made up less than one seventh of all outstanding mortgages in the United States. And the defaults and delinquencies that triggered the crisis were mostly concentrated in subprime mortgages with adjustable interest rates, which accounted for less than one twelfth of all mortgages. Straightforward calculations suggested that even if every subprime mortgage holder defaulted, the losses would be modest and easily absorbed by the capital buffers of most major banks and other creditors. What such calculations missed—what almost everyone missed—was the way mortgages were poised to become a vector of panic throughout the financial system.

KINDLING

When Hank left Goldman Sachs to go to Washington, D.C., in July 2006, the firm had $60 billion worth of unencumbered Treasuries in a virtual "lockbox," not to be used as collateral, not to be risked in trades. Goldman had learned that good times never keep rolling forever, that panics can drag down the responsible along with the reckless, and that in a crisis, liquidity is king.

That was not the prevailing attitude on Wall Street in the early years of the twenty-first century. Financial institutions were bingeing on risk and leverage, borrowing heavily in short-term credit markets—especially "tri-party repo" and "asset-backed commercial paper"—to finance bets on mortgage-related assets and other forms of private credit. Some executives worried about the breakdown of risk management, but those qualms could be expensive during the boom. As Citigroup CEO Chuck Prince observed in 2007: "As long as the music is playing, you've got to get up and dance."

Not all bubbles threaten the stability of the broader financial system. When the dot-com bubble of the late 1990s burst, investors in busted internet stocks like Pets.com lost their money, but there wasn't much of a ripple effect, just a mild recession. The real problems emerge when bubbles are financed with borrowed money, especially when that money can run. And leverage can be alluring, because it's the ultimate profit multiplier. If you spend $100 to buy an asset without leverage, then sell it for $120, your profit is 20 percent. But if you spend only $5 of your own money, borrow the other $95 to buy the same asset, and then sell it for the same $120, the miracle of leverage produces a 400 percent profit.

The downside is that leverage has the same multiplying effect on losses, dramatically increasing "wipeout risk." If you buy that same $100 asset with the same leverage but the asset's value declines below $95, you've lost your entire investment. And if your creditor suddenly demands repayment of the loan, or forces you to post additional collateral, you might have a real problem, especially if you don't have a lockbox full of Treasuries for emergency use only. You might have to sell the asset immediately to avoid default, and if others with similar assets hold similar fire sales, the price of the assets will drop further, triggering more fire sales and margin calls and defaults, and so on down the drain. If you happen to be a financial firm, your creditors might sour on your commercial paper, stop renewing your overnight repo loans, or force you to post more collateral, the modern equivalents of bank runs. That's how panic spread after the housing bubble popped.

Before the crisis of 2008, many large financial institutions were increasingly leveraged, in some cases borrowing more than $30 for every dollar of shareholder capital, affording very limited protection against losses. Increasing amounts of that leverage were in short-term debt that resembled uninsured bank deposits, the kind of runnable debt that uneasy creditors can withdraw at the first hint of danger. And many of these heavily leveraged institutions that were financing themselves with overnight credit had become so big, so interconnected, and so tightly woven into the fabric of modern finance that they would pose a danger to the system if they ever unraveled.

This was all kindling that made the financial system combustible. What made the situation even more explosive—and much more difficult to anticipate or head off—was that many of those institutions were not technically "banks." They behaved like banks, borrowing short and lending long, but they operated outside the commercial banking system, with neither the supervisory oversight nor the safety net our system provides for institutions with commercial bank charters. They faced looser or sometimes nonexistent constraints on their risk taking; they were not financed with insured deposits; and they did not have standing access to the Fed's discount window, which made emergency loans available to commercial banks whenever they were needed. Before the crisis, more than half the leverage in U.S. finance had migrated to these "shadow banks" or "nonbanks"—investment banks like Bear Stearns and Lehman, the mortgage giants Fannie Mae and Freddie Mac, insurance companies like AIG, money market funds, corporate finance arms like GE Capital and GMAC, and even nonbank affiliates of traditional commercial banks.

These firms all engaged in the fragile alchemy of maturity transformation—but without the security of insured deposits that never run, without effective regulatory constraints on their leverage, and without the ability to turn to the Fed if their financing evaporated.

This lack of oversight over nonbanks was particularly dangerous, but the entire U.S. financial regulatory system was creaky and fragmented, a set of overlapping bureaucracies with tribal rivalries. While commercial banks had the most formal oversight, the responsibilities for supervising them were divided among the Fed, the Office of the Comptroller of the Currency (OCC), the Federal Deposit Insurance Corporation (FDIC), the Office of Thrift Supervision (OTS), foreign regulators who helped oversee U.S. affiliates of overseas banks, and various state banking commissions of varying levels of vigilance and competence. In some cases, banks effectively got to choose their own supervisors by changing their legal form—Countrywide reorganized itself as a thrift in order to enjoy the notoriously lenient oversight of the OTS—and often had multiple supervisors with unclear lines of authority.

Outside the commercial banks, oversight was even less stringent. The mortgage giants Fannie Mae and Freddie Mac, known as government-sponsored enterprises, or GSEs, had their own mostly ineffectual Washington regulator. The Securities and Exchange Commission oversaw investment banks, but did not try to constrain their leverage or limit their reliance on short-term funding. The SEC mostly focused on investor protection, as did the Commodity Futures Trading Commission (CFTC), whose purview included many derivatives markets. The Federal Trade Commission, the Fed, and a slew of other federal and state agencies had various financial consumer protection responsibilities, but it wasn't anyone's top priority.

Another critical gap was that none of these agencies was responsible for analyzing or protecting against systemic risk. There

23

was no single regulator responsible for safeguarding or even monitoring the safety and soundness of the system as a whole, rather than the safety and soundness of individual institutions; there wasn't a single supervisor who had visibility into the entire system of nonbanks and banks. Nobody was assessing the general safety of derivatives or overnight funding or other potential threats to stability that cut across institutional or regulatory lines. And while the FDIC had emergency authority to wind down failing commercial banks in a swift and orderly fashion, no one had the authority to step in to avoid a chaotic bankruptcy of a major nonbank during a crisis.

We were all uncomfortable about this, and all three of us established new risk committees and task forces within our institutions before the crisis to try to focus attention on systemic threats. We tried to lean against the prevailing winds of overconfidence, pushing back against the notion that crises were vestiges of the past, calling for more robust risk management and humility about tail risks. But we were not sufficiently creative or forceful in acting to contain those risks, and none of us recognized how they were about to spiral out of control. For all our crisis experience, we still failed to anticipate the worst crisis of our lifetimes. When Ben was later asked what surprised him most about the crisis, he replied: "the crisis." For all our concern about government's inability to ensure the safety and soundness of our messy and complex system, we did not think it was on the edge of panic. We were worried something terrible could happen, but even in the months leading up to it, we didn't foresee how the scenario would unfold. For example, we and most others did not expect short-term wholesale funding to run, because much of that funding was collateralized, providing protection for investors in case of default. We did not anticipate that in panic conditions, investors would not consider even high-quality collateral—which they would have been forced to sell quickly in a rapidly deteriorating market—to be an adequate guarantee.

These failures of anticipation were in part a failure of imagination and in part a failure of institutional organization within the government. There was no overarching agency with responsibility and accountability for monitoring or addressing systemic risk. The patchwork regulatory system was so fragmented that much of what was happening was out of the sight of supervisors, or seen as somebody else's problem. And this crisis was particularly difficult to anticipate because it was the result of not just one or two evident factors, but of a host of complex interactions among many evolving trends: the explosion of financial leverage, the reliance on runnable short-term funding, the migration of risk to the shadow banking system, the rise of "too-big-to-fail" institutions, and the ubiquity of murky derivatives backed by shoddy mortgages. Each of these factors would play an independent role in what unfolded, but their rolling interactions created a particularly dangerous panic.

Of course, we were not alone in our failures; the crisis caught just about everyone by surprise. One lesson for crisis detection is that it's incredibly hard to predict a financial meltdown. Some people might be prescient about some things, but you can't count on prescience as a realistic crisis avoidance strategy.

IT'S HARD TO FIX SOMETHING BEFORE IT BREAKS

The financial system is inherently fragile, but policymakers, including legislators, can make the system more or less fragile. With the benefit of hindsight, it's clear that the government failed to rein in the excesses that would help spark the crisis.

It is now evident, for example, that the government let major financial institutions take on too much risky leverage without insisting that they retain enough capital, the flip side of leverage; the more an institution relies on borrowing, the lower its capital levels, and the greater its exposure to shocks. Capital is the shock absorber that can help an institution withstand losses, retain confidence, and remain solvent during a crisis—and in retrospect, America's financial institutions needed a lot more of it. But that's in retrospect. At the time, banks were easily exceeding their legally mandated capital requirements, and regulators didn't think they could demand that they raise more. The New York Fed did ask the banks it oversaw to run stress tests modeling the potential impact of recessions and other types of shocks, but times had been so good for so long that they couldn't even imagine dark outcomes. Not one bank came up with a scenario that significantly dented its capital buffer. This is the downside of a long period of calm: It can lead to complacency.

It would later become clear that the backward-looking capital regime for banks, designed to protect against the kinds of losses created by relatively mild recent recessions, was not conservative enough. Regulators allowed banks to count too much poor-quality capital toward their required ratios, rather than insisting on loss-absorbing common equity. And supervisors failed to recognize how much leverage banks had hidden in complex derivatives and off-balance-sheet vehicles, which made them look better capitalized than they actually were. This was not usually the result of intentional deception by banks; frequently, the banks themselves were unable to assess the full extent of their exposure to risks. And most bankers were as overconfident as their clients about risks in the housing market.

But while the existing capital regime for commercial banks was too weak, it was nonetheless strong enough to drive trillions of dollars' worth of leverage into the nonbanks that weren't bound by it. Stricter scrutiny of bank capital levels—or for that matter bank liquidity levels or bank reliance on short-term funding— could have driven even more leverage into the undercapitalized shadow banking system, outside the jurisdiction of regulators and the reach of the Fed's safety net. Risk, like love, tends to find a way. That's the paradox, and the inherent danger, of a fragmented regulatory system that sets different standards for institutions that call themselves banks and for institutions that get described by some other name. The most vulnerable firms in this crisis were technically not "banks," although they shared many aspects of the banks' business model. And the most damaging problem with America's capital rules was not that they were too weak, but that they were applied too narrowly. The institutions with the most reckless mortgage-related investments and the least stable funding bases also had the thinnest capital buffers, but they were operating largely outside the reach of the regulatory system.

Ideally, there should have been a stronger and more comprehensive regulatory system, as well as tougher and more proactive regulators, but during the boom, there wasn't much political appetite for stronger financial regulation of any kind. The FDIC's annual report for 2003 included a photo of federal regulators and bank lobbyists taking chain saws and pruning shears to red tape, reflecting the era's dismissive attitudes about bureaucrats meddling with markets. And if the prevailing mood was inhospitable to stricter enforcement of existing regulations focused on banks, it was downright hostile to reforms modernizing those regulations or extending them to nonbanks. The financial industry, flush with profits, defended its prerogatives by pouring more money than ever into Washington lobbying and campaign contributions. Congress had passed a major financial deregulation bill in the Gramm-Leach-Bliley Act of 1999, and the main question before the crisis was whether there would be additional deregulation, not re-regulation.

The three of us learned, as had some of our predecessors, that reform is extremely tough to achieve without a crisis to make the case for it, most vividly with Fannie Mae and Freddie Mac. Those two firms owned or guaranteed half the residential mortgages in the United States. We each expressed concern before the crisis that they were seriously undercapitalized and under-regulated. Market participants assumed the government that chartered them would rescue them if they ever got in trouble, so the companies felt safe piling up leverage—a real example of moral hazard. Ben worked on reforms to strengthen their oversight and rein in their risk taking during his stint as chairman of the Council of Economic Advisers in the Bush White House in 2005, but Fannie and Freddie had powerful friends on Capitol Hill, and the reforms went nowhere. Hank revived the dream of reform when he arrived in Washington in 2006, and eventually worked out a bipartisan compromise with Democrat Barney Frank that would limit speculation by Fannie and Freddie while creating a more powerful regulator and tougher regulatory standards. The bill passed the House but stalled in the Senate. Reform would have to wait until the firms were on the brink of collapse.

The boom was a daunting time to try to improve the stability of the financial system, in part because the system seemed so healthy. Hank led a Treasury effort to create a reorganization plan for the regulatory system, a plan that would provide a blueprint for reform after the crisis, but when it appeared it was largely ignored. Ben set up a financial stability unit at the Fed in Washington and presided over tougher supervisory guidance to limit banks' exposure to commercial real estate and other risks. And Tim launched a series of efforts with other U.S. and foreign regulators designed to improve risk management and focus more attention on the risk of a crisis. In 2005, the New York Fed led an effort with other regulators to force Wall Street's top derivatives dealers to upgrade their antiquated back-office infrastructure, modernizing a system where derivatives orders were routinely faxed to unattended machines and trades often remained unconfirmed for months. But while the changes mitigated a potential source of confusion and panic, they did not reduce the overall leverage in the system. The firms were reluctant to reduce their exposure to risky derivatives because they didn't want to lose market share; recommendations of caution weren't much of a countervailing force against the prevailing mood of optimism. And the Wild West with better plumbing was still the Wild West.

Our modest efforts to shift the system toward responsibility mostly amounted to trying to close the barn door long after the horse had escaped. For example, the Fed finally moved to crack down on no-documentation loans and other egregious mortgage abuses after Ben became chairman, but the crisis had already begun by the time the new regulations wound their way through the rule-making process. Federal regulators also had less scope to rein in irresponsible lending than they would have liked; in 2005, banks and thrifts under federal supervision originated only 20 percent of all subprime mortgages. And once dubious loans were made and securitized, there was no way for regulators to unmake or un-securitize them, or to prevent fear about them from spreading throughout the financial system.

We should have pushed earlier and harder for reform, but a crackdown on mortgage lending would have required a defeat of American political tradition, not to mention the clout of the American real estate industry. There was a long-standing bipartisan consensus that home ownership was essential to the American dream, and the mortgage boom was widely hailed for extending that dream to more Americans than ever, pushing U.S. home ownership rates to a record 69 percent at the height of the boom. Subprime lending in particular was praised for democratizing credit, benefiting low-income families and particularly minorities who had been redlined out of the dream. There was little support in Washington for cracking down on lackadaisical underwriting that was turning renters into home owners, even though some of those new buyers were being exploited.

In general, a regulatory regime that had evolved along with the financial system in the decades after the Depression might have prevented the simultaneous explosions of financial leverage, short-term funding, shadow banking, and even the opaque mortgage-backed derivatives that circulated panic throughout the system. But the actual U.S. regulatory regime was not capable of defusing those bombs, and the politics of the boom was not conducive to reforming the system. There was no momentum for legislative or regulatory efforts to reduce the risk of a crisis that still seemed remote. And even if policymakers had been clairvoyant about that risk, it's hard to see how consenting adults caught up in a mania could have been persuaded to change their risky but legal behaviors.

MISSING THE SPARK

In any case, we were not clairvoyant.

By the spring of 2007, it was clear the housing boom was over and the subprime mortgage market was tanking. But the job market was still strong, and bank capital levels still seemed strong. We didn't believe the bursting of the bubble would have a major financial or economic impact beyond real estate. "The impact on the broader economy and financial markets of the problems in the subprime market seems likely to be contained," Ben testified to Congress in March 2007. Hank also described subprime problems as "largely contained" that spring. The economy did seem healthy, and growth remained decent for most of the year.

Tim gave a speech in Charlotte in March 2007 warning about "what we might call the adverse tail, or the negative extreme." He suggested that a meltdown in the subprime markets could produce "positive feedback dynamics," a vicious cycle where fears about defaults and uncertainty about exposures could lead to fire sales, which could lead to margin calls as collateral backed by mortgages looked shakier and counterparties looked less creditworthy, which could lead to more fire sales. That's exactly what ended up happening. But Tim concluded it wasn't a very likely scenario: "As of now, though, there are few signs that the disruptions in this one sector of the credit markets will have a lasting impact on credit markets as a whole."

By the summer of 2007, however, that vicious cycle was starting to make an appearance. The subprime-mortgage lender Countrywide began running out of cash, and its largest rival went bankrupt. Two hedge funds financed by Bear Stearns—including the Enhanced Leverage Fund, named back when enhanced leverage was something to brag about—collapsed after their mortgage portfolios sputtered.

Our assumption that the carnage in subprime would bring some healthy discipline to a chaotic sliver of the credit markets without much broader damage seemed reasonable, given what we knew at the time. But it was too reasonable. Our analyses focusing on the modest size and scope of subprime left out the unquantifiable variable of fear. We didn't foresee how the complexity and opacity of mortgage-backed securities would lead creditors and investors to run from anything and anyone associated with mortgages, and not just subprime mortgages. We didn't anticipate how bad news about one segment of the housing market could create what the economist Gary Gorton has dubbed the *E. coli* effect, where rumors about a few incidents of tainted hamburger frighten consumers into abandoning all meat rather than trying to figure out which meat in which stores in which parts of the country is actually tainted.

Subprime was a problem, but if it hadn't triggered a financial panic it would have been a problem just for subprime borrowers and subprime lenders. More than half the U.S. housing losses would happen *after* the failures and near-failures of September 2008. Without the panic, the relatively isolated problems in subprime really would have been contained. Fear turned those isolated sparks into an inferno.

But the psychological roots of the inferno didn't make it less dangerous. Fire prevention had failed. Now the fate of the system would depend on firefighting.

CHAPTER TWO

THE FIRST FLAMES:

August 2007–March 2008

ON AUGUST 9, 2007, BNP PARIBAS, FRANCE'S LARGEST BANK, announced a freeze on withdrawals from three funds that held securities backed by U.S. subprime mortgages, blaming the "complete evaporation of liquidity" in the markets for those securities. We knew enough about crises to know that this felt like a crisis, although we had no idea it would metastasize into the worst crisis in generations.

What made the news so unnerving was not merely that securities backed by subprime mortgages were losing value, but that BNP Paribas said it had no idea how to assign them any value, because no one was buying them "regardless of their quality." That kind of inchoate fear and uncertainty is what panics are made of. Banks were hoarding cash, the rates they were charging each other to borrow were spiking, and skittish investors were pulling money out of other funds to make sure their cash didn't get frozen as well.

In the early phase of any crisis, policymakers have to calibrate how forcefully to respond to a situation they don't yet entirely understand. Governments that routinely ride to the rescue at the first hint of trouble can create real moral hazard, encouraging reckless speculation, propping up nonviable "zombie banks," and setting up the financial system to fall from a higher cliff in the future. But underreacting can be even costlier and more damaging than overreacting. Ben's academic research had shown how inaction by timid central bankers made the Great Depression great. Tim had seen while fighting financial crises in Latin America and Asia how government delay and half measures can accelerate panics. Unfortunately, crises don't announce themselves as either idiosyncratic brush fires that will burn themselves out or systemic nightmares with the potential to burn down the core of the financial system. Policymakers need to figure it out as they go along.

The early stages of a financial crisis are not the memorable stages. Today, Americans remember the government interventions to rescue Bear Stearns, Fannie Mae, Freddie Mac, AIG, and ultimately the entire financial system, but in the first phase of our firefighting we quietly said no to the firms that asked for help. Initially, the Federal Reserve responded with traditional and then less traditional central-bank lending to try to restore liquidity to the system. The more dramatic escalations would come later, after the fire started burning hotter. The stability of the financial system began to erode long before most families could feel the impact of the Great Recession, and even our modest early interventions were criticized as misguided overreactions that would rescue the reckless and ratchet up moral hazard.

The three of us would work together as a team throughout the crisis, talking to one another every day, usually multiple times. Since the initial problem was a shortage of liquidity, and because at the time the Treasury had very limited financial authority, almost all the early action had to come from the Fed.

THE BAGEHOT PLAYBOOK

In normal times, the main role of a central bank is to lower or raise interest rates—giving the economy a boost to promote growth or hitting the brakes to avoid inflation. But when confidence erodes and credit markets seize up, central banks can also be the "lender of last resort," providing liquidity to solvent firms when private lenders won't. The Federal Reserve's lender-of-last-resort function, known as the "discount window," offers emergency liquidity to any commercial bank facing a cash crunch. Access to the discount window is intended to allow banks to meet withdrawals by private creditors without having to dump their assets in a destabilizing fire sale. Along with deposit insurance, as well as the FDIC's tools for managing the failure of an insolvent depository institution in an orderly fashion, the federal government had fairly strong protections for the traditional banking system.

Unfortunately, the traditional banking system no longer dominated American finance, and it wasn't the epicenter of the problems in American finance. But in the early moments of the crisis, the discount window was the natural place to start.

The British journalist Walter Bagehot wrote *Lombard Street*, the bible of central banking, in 1873, and it's still a key part of the crisis response playbook. Bagehot recognized that the only way to stop a run is to show the world there's no need to run, to make credit easily available to solvent firms until the panic subsides: "Lend freely, boldly, and so that the public may feel you mean to go on lending." The loans should be expensive enough that they'll remain attractive only as long as the crisis lasts—Bagehot advised "a penalty rate"—and they should be secured by solid collateral to protect the central bank in case of default. But the goal should be to make public money available when private money isn't, to push back against panic and stabilize credit. Ben's research had shown how clogged credit channels can devastate an economy, and how the Fed's reluctance to provide liquidity in the 1930s had helped create the Great Depression.

The BNP Paribas news created a classic liquidity crunch: Money fled to safer assets as uneasy creditors got pickier about collateral and shortened the terms of loans. The European Central Bank promptly injected $130 billion into frozen credit markets by buying securities on the open market. The Fed poured in a further $62 billion by buying Treasuries and issued a statement encouraging banks to borrow from the discount window. Even those textbook initial steps were criticized as too much too soon. Bank of England governor Mervyn King called out the ECB and the Fed for overreacting to blips in the markets. A month later, the Bank of England would provide similar liquidity after his country's first bank run in 150 years. Inside the Fed, several Federal Open Market Committee (FOMC) members wanted to attach harsh conditions to discount window loans to avoid moral hazard. But Ben and Tim didn't want to add to the stigma the banks already associated with Fed loans. We didn't want banks to stay away from the discount window; we wanted them to take the Fed's money and lend it out.

The general infusion of liquidity helped bring some calm to the markets, but even without onerous conditions, the Fed's come-and-get-it message did not attract banks to the discount window. The loans are supposed to be confidential, but banks were afraid they'd look weak and desperate if markets got wind that they had paid a penalty rate. That's the essence of the "stigma" problem, which makes institutions reluctant to take government help even when that help is essential to the stability of the broader system. The Fed tried to make discount window borrowing more attractive by reducing the penalty rate and extending the length of time for which banks could borrow. The Fed had never lost a dollar on a discount window loan, so this felt like an extremely modest escalation. But many inflation hawks and other skeptics inside as well as outside the Fed thought the central bank should let the market adjust on its own, rather than interfere with a deleveraging process they saw as healthy and necessary. "I realize the urge to act—to do something or at least to be seen doing something—can be irresistible," said Jeffrey Lacker, the president of the Richmond Fed. "But I think that we need to avoid the urge to play Mr. Fix-It."

But the Fed exists to act when credit markets freeze. Economies wither when people can't get home loans, car loans, student loans, or business loans. The hawks believed inflation was a more serious danger, and kept believing that even as the crisis heated up. From Ben's perspective, though, the Fed's obsession with inflation and moral hazard during a credit crunch had already created one depression. He didn't intend to let it create another.

These debates were an early indicator of the messy politics of financial crises. French president Nicolas Sarkozy advised Hank to find a convenient villain to deflect the inevitable public backlash; he suggested scapegoating the ratings agencies that had slapped triple-A ratings on shoddy securities. "You need a simple story, and I know you won't want to blame the bankers," Sarkozy teased him. But we didn't think our job was assigning blame for the crisis. We just wanted to fix it.

The Bagehot prescription was the necessary response to a liquidity crunch. We hoped it would help to calm market fears and stabilize the situation, without artificially sustaining the financial boom. We didn't intend to provide any more government support for the financial system than was necessary to protect the overall economy.

Capitalism depends on creative destruction. Someone builds a better mousetrap, so incumbent mousetrap makers must adapt or die. Automakers wipe out buggy-whip manufacturers, then the market determines which automakers survive. The same principles normally apply to financial firms. The strong, nimble, and reliable thrive, while the imprudent and mismanaged get devoured. Failure is usually a healthy phenomenon, instilling discipline in survivors. Early in a crisis, the default assumption should be that private firms face the consequences of their mistakes, even though the firms often clamor for help, and even though policymakers are often pressured to take action to prove they "get it." Not all bubbles or even all crashes end in catastrophe. It's fine to let a financial fire burn for a while, as long as the damage is containable; it can clear out underbrush and improve the resilience of the forest. Some financial losses are inevitable after an asset bubble, and it's counterproductive to try to prevent all deleveraging or sustain the unsustainable.

But severe financial panics are not usually self-correcting, and fires can burn out of control when fear and uncertainty gain too much momentum. When policymakers are too slow to act—because they don't think the dangers are that great, because they're too concerned about avoiding moral hazard, or because they're overly focused on the political fallout—panic can consume the prudent and strong as well as the reckless and weak, innocent bystanders as well as overleveraged speculators. And panic is contagious. Just as Mexico's debt problems in the 1990s stoked fears about bonds issued by other emerging Latin American economies, the so-called Tequila Effect, defaults in subprime in 2007 raised suspicions about somewhat safer Alt-A mortgages and even prime mortgages, made to the strongest borrowers. There's a fuzzy and hard-to-discern line between a healthy adjustment that inflicts pain on the irresponsible and a panic that imposes indiscriminate damage throughout the system. Systemic crises are not the time for free-market absolutism or moral-hazard purism, because of the serious risks they pose to lending, jobs, and incomes, and because systemic crises rarely end without government substituting sovereign credit for private credit, putting some public money at risk, and, as a consequence, creating some moral hazard. It's messy, it's distasteful, but it's preferable to a financial implosion that sends the broader economy into a tailspin.

There will always be investor pressure on central banks to do more to boost markets, and there will always be political pressure on central banks to do less, to teach speculators a lesson. Ben didn't want to create a "Bernanke put" by sending a message of unlimited central bank support for troubled markets, but he definitely didn't want financial disruptions to choke off credit and reprise the 1930s. The challenge was figuring out how much support the financial system truly needed, as opposed to how much it wanted.

Policymakers can't trust everything they hear from market participants. Even the most credible tend to "talk their book," whether consciously or not. But our Bloomberg terminals didn't have all the information necessary to understand the growing risks in the market. We were on the phone constantly with our counterparts in other agencies and other countries. And we talked regularly to the executives running financial firms, large and small, in New York and across the country. Sometimes they gave us market color about what their customers and bankers were thinking. Sometimes we just needed to hear how much fear was in their voices. Sometimes they professed confidence, sometimes they pleaded for assistance. Often they didn't know that much about the risks ahead. We had to sort through all the confusion and self-interest and decide what was in the public interest.

The first firm to ask for direct help from the Fed was Countrywide Financial, a $200 billion poster child for the excesses that fueled the housing boom. It had originated one of every five U.S. mortgages in 2006, but by the start of the crisis, the cost of insuring its debt against default had soared 800 percent in a month. CEO Angelo Mozilo insisted his firm was fine, accusing analysts who warned about its dwindling liquidity of shouting "fire" in a crowded theater. But as Bagehot wrote, bluster rarely restores confidence: "Every banker knows that if he has to *prove* that he is worthy of credit, however good may be his arguments, in fact his credit is gone."

Countrywide was a case study in just about all the vulnerabilities in the system: overreliance on lower-quality mortgages, regulatory arbitrage, and especially runnable short-term financing. First some of its creditors stopped "rolling over" its commercial paper, forcing it to sell off assets to pay them back. Then on the night of August 15, it looked like the Bank of New York Mellon (BoNY), Countrywide's clearing bank, would refuse to "unwind" its $45 billion repo book—that is, take temporary responsibility for Countrywide's maturing obligations while new lenders were being lined up—which would have signaled its unwillingness to guarantee Countrywide's stability. (Repos are a form of short-term debt, widely used by financial firms. They are not government guaranteed, but borrowers put up some of their financial assets as collateral.) That vote of no confidence would have triggered a much larger fire sale of the securities Countrywide was using as collateral, and probably a run on Countrywide.

BoNY said it would unwind only if the Fed indemnified it for any intraday losses it suffered from its exposure to Countrywide. But that essentially would have required the Fed to guarantee the entire repo market, since firms in similar quandaries would have expected similar treatment. Meanwhile, Mozilo wanted the Fed to let Countrywide's cash-starved nonbank affiliates borrow from the discount window. But that would have required invoking Section 13(3) of the Federal Reserve Act, which authorizes emergency actions in "unusual and exigent circumstances." It hadn't been invoked since the Depression, and Countrywide still had access to an $11.5 billion credit line.

Ben and Tim decided not to intervene. It was early in the triage process, and we didn't want to send a message that the government would backstop any big firm in trouble. And the Fed was a lender of *last* resort; we couldn't justify helping a firm that could still help itself. Countrywide finally agreed late that night to draw down its credit line and upgrade its collateral, so BoNY agreed to unwind. Soon Bank of America would buy Countrywide and transfer its problems to its own balance sheet.

Still, the Countrywide drama foreshadowed the problems brewing outside traditional banks, and our limited ability to fix them. It was also a troubling illustration of the danger of wholesale funding. In one turbulent week, the spreads between yields on Treasuries and asset-backed commercial paper had skyrocketed eightfold, from 35 basis points to 280 (or, from 0.35 percentage points to 2.80). We had just seen how the \$1.2 trillion commercial paper market and the \$2.3 trillion repo market could be vulnerable to runs.

BEYOND BAGEHOT

The Fed's come-and-get-it approach did not end up luring many banks to the discount window early that fall—partly because the stigma of borrowing from the Fed persisted, partly because the turmoil eased. The stock market hit a record high, interbank lending rates stabilized, and Lehman completed its misguided acquisition of the real estate firm Archstone-Smith. So far, the crisis had played out like a rerun of 1998, when the giant hedge fund Long-Term Capital Management's demise produced widespread anxiety, but, after a modest intervention by the Fed, no widespread damage.

But this calm did not last. First Merrill Lynch announced the biggest write-down of troubled assets in Wall Street history and ousted its CEO. Then Citigroup broke Merrill's record and ousted its CEO, the one who had said banks needed to keep dancing while the music was playing. The size of the losses was scary, but psychologically, the sense that financial giants had no idea what ugly surprises were hidden in their own balance sheets was scarier. Merrill's write-down was twice as large as it had predicted three weeks earlier. Citi's write-down was seven times as large as it had predicted on its last earnings call. Both firms revealed huge new subprime exposures they evidently hadn't noticed before. They looked oblivious, and gave the impression that losses were exploding all around them.

The sources of the losses were also unsettling. Merrill's came mostly from "super-senior CDOs," one of the supposedly safer forms of mortgage securities. But they were still mortgage securities, so investors and creditors who had bought them or accepted them as collateral without much analysis began selling them and rejecting them as collateral with just as little analysis. The sudden toxicity of super-seniors was a sign that mania was flipping into panic, that markets were simply frightened of the word "mortgage." Citi faced similar problems with the $1.2 trillion of "structured investment vehicles" and other assets it had stashed outside its balance sheet. SIVs, which had sources of funding separate from the sponsoring banks, had been considered safe during the boom. But now that a few SIVs with subprime exposure had failed, shaken investors were fleeing all SIVs, forcing firms like Citi to bring their troubled assets back on balance sheet to avoid a reputational hit.

Hank tried to ease the problem by arranging a "Super SIV," a privately financed investment fund that would buy SIV assets in order to avoid destabilizing fire sales. But the big banks had too many of their own problems to finance it, and without government backing the effort fizzled. The Fed also forced Citi to start conserving capital by ordering the bank to reduce its dividend. And together we pressured other troubled institutions to raise new capital. Citi raised $20 billion over the next few months, mostly from sovereign wealth funds in the Middle East and Asia. Morgan Stanley and Merrill also brought in foreign investors, who got to watch their new stakes in prestigious Wall Street firms crater almost immediately.

The *E. coli* effect was beginning to manifest itself, as investors and creditors began to shun entire classes of financial products whether they were contaminated with subprime or not, which depressed their prices and made them even more toxic. It was as if avoiding meat caused *E. coli* to spread. Fear was overwhelming reason, because nobody knew when bad news would cause the next paroxysm of fire sales. It felt rational to assume the worst. The troubled securities would all be worth something someday; not all mortgages would default, and the ones that did would recoup some of their value in foreclosure sales. But at a moment when nobody wanted the securities, their prices were dropping without regard to their underlying quality.

This was starting to look like a problem the traditional Bagehot playbook could not solve. The Fed's conventional tools, which mostly consisted of loans against collateral to U.S. commercial banks, were proving ineffective in unclogging important parts of the credit system. The few banks that dared to visit the discount window weren't lending to other financial institutions or anyone else, and many of the institutions in trouble were not commercial banks. In December, the Fed decided to launch two novel efforts to boost liquidity, taking a tentative step beyond basic Bagehot into uncharted waters.

The first was the Term Auction Facility (TAF), a program designed to overcome the stigma of the discount window by not only lengthening the terms of the loans but auctioning them to eligible banks, rather than lending at a fixed rate. Borrowers would pay a market rate determined by auction, not a penalty rate, so they wouldn't seem so desperate if word of their loans leaked. Within a year, the Fed would be lending five times as much through the TAF as the discount window. The second innovation was swap lines that the Fed established with the ECB and other foreign central banks, so they in turn could on-lend dollars to private banks in their own countries. (They were called swaps because the Fed got foreign currency in exchange for its dollars, as well as guarantees of repayment by the foreign central banks, which are government institutions.) Since the dollar is effectively the global currency, making dollars available to foreign central banks was an important step toward calming global markets. A year later, the Fed would have more than $500 billion in swaps outstanding, enshrining it as the lender of last resort to the world.

The auction loans and swaps did help ease the liquidity crunch in the U.S. financial system, but the underlying conditions were getting worse, and the breakdown of the credit engine was starting to damage the broader economy, worsening the stresses created by the unwinding of the housing bubble. Hank warned the White House in December that the economy was hitting a wall. (The official arbiters of the business cycle at the National Bureau of Economic Research would later determine that a recession started that month.) The feedback loop of fear and fire sales within Wall Street was contributing to a feedback loop of credit contractions and business contractions between Wall Street and Main Street. Worsening financial conditions were creating worse economic conditions, which in turn were accelerating the subprime meltdown and the financial panic. Ultimately, we wouldn't be able to stabilize the financial system without stabilizing the economy, and vice versa. To put out the fire, we'd have to do both.

In 2007, the Fed provided a little monetary stimulus to the economy by cutting short-term interest rates from 5.25 percent to 4.25 percent, but only a little. Ben had led the Fed with a deferential consensus-based approach, trying to get the institution to speak with one voice. But the Fed was falling behind the curve of the crisis, and in 2008, Ben pushed monetary stimulus more aggressively, overriding the objections of the FOMC's inflation hawks. The Fed cut rates to 2.25 percent by March, trying to provide fuel for the sputtering economy. The Fed would cut rates faster than any other central bank during the crisis, and in retrospect it probably should have cut them even faster. In a crisis, however, monetary policy can only do so much, especially when the banking system and the public are already overleveraged and panic conditions are constraining credit.

Meanwhile, Hank led a White House push for a jolt of Keynesian fiscal stimulus in January 2008, building support for a package of temporary tax cuts that would help offset the contraction in private demand. He negotiated a bipartisan deal with House Speaker Nancy Pelosi and House Minority Leader John Boehner that consisted of $150 billion in tax cuts with no new spending, as President Bush had proposed. The compromise directed most of the tax cuts to working families—including tax credits for low-income families that don't pay income taxes but do pay other federal taxes—in the way Democrats wanted. The deal sailed through Congress, Bush signed it in mid-February, and the first checks would go out in April. It was a modest response to a slowdown, only 1 percent of GDP, but it was among the swiftest responses Congress ever approved. It also proved the legislative process could still function, while giving Hank a chance to forge relationships on Capitol Hill that would come in handy later.

Still, the fire kept advancing. Among those feeling the heat were the so-called monoline insurers, which had expanded their traditional business of insuring municipal bonds to guaranteeing, for a fee, subprime mortgage securities and CDOs. Losses to monolines led investors to begin doubting the other securities they insured, including municipal bonds. The Fed faced pressure to help all kinds of companies with exposures to mortgages. Ben even personally heard out the head of Thornburg Mortgage, Larry Goldstone, who wanted the Fed to invoke its 13(3) powers to provide an emergency loan after his repo lenders rejected his collateral.

The Fed turned down these requests, but Ben and Tim were actively exploring new ways to ease the pressures on the rest of the system, steps that would go beyond lending to banks. In March 2008, the Fed unveiled the Term Securities Lending Facility, an innovative new program that would finally extend liquidity to nonbanks, allowing nonbank firms, including the five major investment banks, the ability to swap less-liquid for more-liquid collateral. The TSLF required the Fed to invoke its Section 13(3) emergency lending powers for the first time since 1936, but Ben told his board it was vital to address the cash crunch in the shadow banking system: "This is unusual, but so are market conditions." The Fed approved the program on March 10, but it wouldn't be ready for two and a half weeks.

By then, market conditions would be much more unusual.

CHAPTER THREE

THE FIRE SPREADS:

March 2008–September 2008

HANK REVIEWED A DRAFT OF AN ECONOMIC SPEECH PRESI-dent Bush planned to deliver in mid-March, and he liked it. He thought it would help reassure the nation of the administration's determination to end the crisis. But he did recommend one fix: Don't say there will be "no bailouts." The president was taken aback.

"We're not going to do a bailout, are we?" he asked.

Hank didn't want to, and he hoped there wouldn't be a need to, but the turbulence in the markets was getting worse every day.

"Mr. President, the fact is, the whole system is so fragile we don't know what we might have to do if a financial institution is about to go down," Hank said.

In fact, a major financial institution was already on the verge: Bear Stearns, an eighty-five-year-old investment bank with $400 billion in assets. Like Countrywide, it now faced a crisis of confidence, in part over its mortgage exposures. Creditors had stopped rolling over its commercial paper, repo lenders were demanding more collateral, and hedge funds were closing their brokerage accounts with the firm. Neither the Fed nor the Treasury oversaw Bear; its regulator was the SEC, an enforcement agency that focused on investor protections, not safety and soundness. But Bear was so inextricably enmeshed in the financial system that its failure threatened to tear the system apart, and we couldn't ignore the threat just because it began outside our jurisdiction.

The collapse of Bear Stearns on March 14 would mark an inflection point in the crisis, exposing the system to its greatest peril and putting America's emergency arsenal to its sternest test since the Depression. The Fed crossed a Rubicon by intervening to prevent the implosion of a nonbank. The Bear rescue did help avert the cascade of financial defaults and economic pain that we would later see after the collapse of Lehman Brothers, and it helped buy six months of relative calm. But it was not particularly comforting even at the time. We would not have been able to prevent a chaotic failure if JPMorgan Chase hadn't been willing to buy Bear and guarantee the vast majority of its obligations. And we knew that Bear wasn't the only overleveraged and interconnected nonbank at risk of a run. Seven months into the crisis, the Bear drama was a sobering reality check about the frailty of the system, the limits of our powers, and the potential for catastrophe in the near future.

BEAR STEARNS: TOO INTERCONNECTED TO FAIL

Unfettered by the capital requirements and other rules constraining commercial banks, Bear Stearns had been aggressive in using leverage during the boom and enjoyed five straight years of record earnings. But by the week of March 10, a run on Bear was under way, and it was hard to imagine how the run could stop on its own. After all, an investment bank that doesn't have the confidence of its clients or the markets doesn't have much of anything.

From the market's perspective, Bear was mostly just a collection of fragile businesses and risky assets. Trading businesses depend on trust, and once people started doubting whether Bear was certain to meet its obligations, they were rushing to take their business elsewhere, which was making Bear even less trustworthy.

Bear Stearns was the nation's seventeenth-largest financial institution, the smallest of the five stand-alone investment banks. But it was twice the size of Countrywide, and far more intertwined with the financial system, with 5,000 trading counterparties and 750,000 open derivatives contracts. It did business with banks, brokerage houses, hedge funds, pension funds, governments, and corporations—and counterparties were scrambling to reduce their exposures to Bear while trying to deduce who else might be exposed to it. The system had already been weakened by seven months of slow burn, and it was disturbing to imagine the hysteria Bear could unleash by defaulting on its obligations—fire sales of its collateral; frantic unwinding of its derivatives trades; a meltdown of the repo market; a likely run on Lehman, the next-weakest investment bank; perhaps even the collapse of the mortgage giants Fannie Mae and Freddie Mac. By Thursday night, March 13, Bear was toast; its cash reserves had dwindled from $18 billion to $2 billion in four days, and it planned to file for bankruptcy in the morning.

At first, we didn't think we could prevent a bankruptcy. The FDIC had the power to wind down insolvent banks in an orderly fashion while standing behind their obligations, but the federal government had no orderly resolution regime for nonbanks that could avoid the chaos of default. We thought the Fed's response would be limited to injecting more liquidity into the markets to contain the damage from an unavoidable collapse, what Tim called putting "foam on the runway" to try to prevent the fire from spreading after Bear crashed and burned.

Bagehot's tool kit of central bank lending had limited value in preventing a run on a weak institution, and the government's other emergency authorities just weren't as broad as people assumed. The Treasury couldn't do much without congressional authorization, while the Fed's authority was limited mostly to lending against solid collateral; neither the Fed nor the Treasury had powers to guarantee obligations, invest capital, or buy illiquid assets to stop a run on a bank. The Term Securities Lending Facility (TSLF) was not yet in place, and the Fed didn't have a standing facility to lend to an investment bank like Bear. It did have Section 13(3), so it could fund nonbanks in "unusual and exigent circumstances." But 13(3) was not a magic wand that could make an insolvent company viable, a ruined brand marketable, or toxic assets valuable.

In a panic, it can be difficult to tell whether a troubled firm is truly insolvent. Markets are not always right or rational, and it's always possible that securities nobody wants during a spiral of fear will turn out to be solid once confidence returns. That's when government loans and liquidity can help a fundamentally viable firm make its payments and avoid getting dragged down with the weak. But Bear's decline, so much faster and sharper than the declines of similar firms, suggested its weakness was real and extreme. In any case, the Fed had not seen Bear's books and had no basis for concluding it was a solvent victim of a misguided run. The SEC, which did have access to Bear's books, did not seem to believe that, either. Based on what we knew, we did not believe a loan against the eroding value of Bear's assets and businesses would succeed in saving the firm. By lending into the accelerating run, we feared that the Fed would succeed only in financing the exits of the few short-term creditors that hadn't already exited, without preventing Bear's ultimate collapse and the chaos that would entail.

In the predawn hours of March 14, the New York Fed staff came up with a stopgap plan to invoke 13(3) and get Bear to the weekend alive: a Fed loan to its clearing bank JPMorgan Chase, which would pass the money on to Bear, which would secure the loan with assets that its repo lenders would no longer accept as collateral. Basically, the Fed would be Bear's repo lender for a day. Many of our colleagues were uneasy with this move, which appeared to suggest we could guarantee the obligations of a failing nonbank, but we agreed it would at least give us the weekend to search for an alternative to disaster. "You can take out that line in your speech about 'no bailouts,'" Hank quipped when he informed the president.

Because we didn't think the Fed could lend enough against Bear's weakened collateral to save the firm as an independent entity, we still needed to find a buyer for Bear to prevent it from disintegrating when the markets opened on Monday. JPMorgan quickly emerged as the only potential savior with the credibility to stand behind Bear's trades, and CEO Jamie Dimon insisted he'd do a deal only if the Fed took on some of the risk of Bear's mortgage assets. So on Sunday night, the Federal Reserve invoked 13(3) again for another creative interpretation of the Fed's power to lend against collateral.

JPMorgan agreed to buy Bear for $2 a share, an offer Dimon later increased to $10 to make sure Bear's shareholders didn't scuttle the merger and plunge the system back into chaos. That was vital, because JPMorgan also agreed to take the risk of guaranteeing Bear's book while waiting for the merger to close, the panic-relieving backstop the Fed didn't have the authority to provide. But the Fed would lend $30 billion to a new entity it dubbed Maiden Lane, which would then buy $30 billion worth of Bear's securities from JPMorgan. Under 13(3), the Fed can only make a loan when it is "secured to the satisfaction" of the Reserve Bank making the loan, a rather hazy standard. A team from the investment firm BlackRock that analyzed the assets JPMorgan wanted to leave behind advised us there was a reasonable chance the loan would be repaid without losses within a few years. Ben and Tim decided that if the Treasury indemnified the Fed against any potential losses, the Fed would be satisfied, and Hank readily agreed.

But then the Treasury's lawyers told Hank he couldn't indemnify the Fed; we were learning just how little power the Treasury had in a crisis. So Tim asked Hank to write a letter supporting the Fed loan and noting that if it lost money, the Fed would simply contribute fewer profits to the Treasury. Hank called it his "all money is green" letter, and while it didn't mean much legally—the Fed routinely remits all of its earnings above its operating costs to the Treasury—it did implicate the Treasury and the executive branch in the Fed's momentous decision. We wanted everyone to know we were in this together.

At the same time, the Fed invoked 13(3) again to launch a more aggressive lending program for investment banks called the Primary Dealer Credit Facility (PDCF), which would accept a greater range of collateral, including riskier assets, than the TSLF. We hoped the Bear intervention would settle down the markets, but we also knew that Lehman Brothers had problems similar to Bear's, and that Merrill Lynch, Morgan Stanley, and even Goldman Sachs might need easier access to the emergency safety net.

The Bear intervention did calm the markets, but it also provided a searing dose of the politics of crisis response. Many politicians and pundits accused us of overreacting to the Darwinian rhythms of capitalism, arguing that the economic impact of an investment bank's failure would be modest—an argument that would be disproved by Lehman's failure six months later. Liberals and conservatives alike attacked us for squandering taxpayer dollars to bail out incompetent bankers. Moral hazard purists warned that we were encouraging excessive risk taking; Republican senator Jim Bunning of Kentucky denounced us as socialists. Even former Fed chairman Paul Volcker said the Fed's actions "extend to the very edge of its lawful and implied powers," which was accurate—we had been careful not to go over the edge—but did not sound like a compliment. We were realizing that we faced a dual challenge: figuring out the right thing to do, and explaining why it was the right thing to do.

One thing we struggled to explain about the Bear rescue was who exactly got rescued. The intervention did ensure that Bear's creditors and counterparties got paid in full, so they would stop running, and so creditors and counterparties of similarly situated firms wouldn't start running. During a crisis, anything that increases uncertainty about repayment of creditors can be a signal to stampede. But Bear itself didn't get bailed out. The firm ceased to exist. Its senior executives lost their jobs and much of their wealth. Its shareholders did receive more than the zero dollars the firm would have been worth in bankruptcy, but 95 percent less than the firm was worth at its peak in early 2007. All interventions create some moral hazard, but it was hard to see how Bear's fate would have encouraged other firms to emulate its reckless approach. And of course, the eventual run on Lehman would prove that markets were not confident the government would ride to the rescue again.

In any case, we did not squander taxpayer dollars; the Bear loan was ultimately repaid and produced a $2.5 billion return for the government. But the point of the loan was not to make money; it was to prevent the messy collapse of a systemically important firm and the inevitable economic damage that would have followed. It's still frightening to think of the chain reaction Bear's failure might have produced at a time when we had not yet stabilized Fannie Mae and Freddie Mac, which were propping up what was left of the U.S. mortgage market. Doing nothing was still an option when Countrywide was flailing, but Bear really was too interconnected to fail, and after seven months in the fire the financial system really was too fragile to handle its failure.

We did not feel triumphant after the Bear rescue. We felt uncomfortable. The episode demonstrated how confidence in heavily leveraged and loosely regulated nonbanks with too much short-term funding could disappear in a heartbeat. And Bear wasn't the only financial institution that had borrowed too much and too short with too little oversight, or invested too much in sketchy mortgages and structured credit products that nobody trusted anymore. Hank was so worried about Fannie Mae and Freddie Mac that on the frenetic Sunday of Bear weekend, he took time out to arrange a call with their CEOs and their regulator, using Bear's example to pressure the firms to raise more capital. Suspicions were also mounting in the markets that Lehman would be "next," which can be a self-fulfilling prophecy for a financial firm. Lehman was 75 percent bigger than Bear, with more real estate exposure, an even larger derivatives book, and $200 billion in repo financing, so in many ways it looked like an even more inviting target for a run.

In fact, the entire business model that produced Bear was now under suspicion; after Bear, Hank had to persuade several European finance ministers not to urge their banks to stop dealing with any of the four surviving U.S. investment banks. Now that the Fed was lending to investment banks, it finally gained the power to examine their books. The results were not reassuring. Fed stress tests found that Lehman, Merrill Lynch, Morgan Stanley, and Goldman Sachs were all vulnerable to runs on their wholesale funding, and that Lehman would need $84 billion in additional liquidity to survive a Bear-style scenario. We pushed all four firms to reduce their leverage, find longer-term sources of funding, and raise more capital, but investment banks did not look like an alluring investment at the time.

We had worked well together in harrowing circumstances to devise a solution for Bear. But we had also gotten lucky. If JPMorgan hadn't been willing to guarantee Bear's book and absorb most of Bear's assets, the system might well have imploded that March. Volcker was right that the Fed had pushed the limits of its powers, and the ad hoc rescue had exposed the inadequacy of those powers. The U.S. government still had no way to inject capital into a struggling firm, buy its assets, or guarantee its liabilities, which meant it had no way to stop a full-blown run; if the firm was a nonbank, there wouldn't even be a way to wind it down safely to avoid default. The combination of the Fed's support for JPMorgan's acquisition of Bear Stearns and the Fed's new PDCF lending facility for investment banks helped build expectations that we had the will and the means to prevent the failure of the other investment banks, but in reality the government's capacity to do so was limited.

Shortly after Bear, Ben and Hank went to see Barney Frank, the Democratic chairman of the House Financial Services Committee, to explain that Lehman could face a similar situation, so we needed emergency resolution authority to prevent a disorderly failure of an investment bank in case we couldn't find a buyer like JPMorgan. Barney explained that the politics would be impossible before the November elections unless we trumpeted our fears about Lehman and persuaded Congress its collapse would be devastating to America. We knew he was right about the politics—any legislation increasing the authority of crisis managers would be savaged as a bailout bill—and we also knew that alarmist rhetoric could end up rattling the markets and precipitating the failure we were trying to avoid. We would have to make do with limited tools until disaster made our case for more.

We felt like we were fighting the crisis with duct tape and baling wire. The markets calmed down a bit after Bear, and we hoped they would stay calm for a while. But as Tim liked to say, hope is not a strategy.

FANNIE MAE AND FREDDIE MAC: FIRING THE BAZOOKA

On July 11, there was a run on an American bank—not a metaphorical run, like the one on Bear Stearns, but an actual run to an actual building, like the one in *It's a Wonderful Life*. After the FDIC seized IndyMac Bank, a California thrift formerly affiliated with Countrywide and similarly rash in its approach to real estate, panicked depositors lined up outside and demanded their money back. The FDIC guaranteed deposits up to $100,000, so most of them had nothing to worry about. But the images of panic from the largest U.S. bank failure since the savings and loan crisis of the 1980s made national news. The next week, fearful depositors withdrew more than $1 billion a day from Washington Mutual, a thrift even larger than IndyMac with similar mortgage exposures. Panic is a communicable disease.

IndyMac's failure was a sign that the fire was burning hotter again, but it didn't seem to threaten the core of the system. Our main concerns that week were Fannie Mae and Freddie Mac, the government-sponsored mortgage giants that together were more than fifty times the size of IndyMac—and more than four times the size of Bear. They held or guaranteed more than $5 trillion worth of mortgage debt, and were also the last major source of mortgage financing in the United States, backing three of every four new home loans. That meant their collapse would halt production of new mortgages and crush the already battered housing market, which would mean more foreclosures on Main Street and more panic about mortgage securities on Wall Street. Fannie Mae and Freddie Mac were undeniably systemic, and they were hemorrhaging.

There was no standing authority that would enable the government to save Fannie Mae and Freddie Mac; Hank would have to persuade Congress to legislate that, forcing our crisis response into the center of the political fray. We would end up essentially nationalizing two of America's most significant firms, another intervention that would have been inconceivable in normal times. Again, our actions were deeply unpopular, but again, we believe they staved off calamitous defaults—and again, they ended up turning a sizable profit for taxpayers while doing more than any other public or private action to help resuscitate the housing market. But while the takeover of Fannie Mae and Freddie Mac was absolutely necessary and broke the panic over their securities, it did not break the panic in the broader system. If anything, it sent an unintended message that the system was more fragile than ever.

Fannie Mae and Freddie Mac were strange hybrids. They had federal charters to promote affordable home ownership, but they were also lucrative private firms that dominated the secondary mortgage market. These government-sponsored enterprises, or GSEs, had deep influence with both parties in Washington and exploited assumptions that the government would never let them fail to borrow heavily at below-market rates without much of a capital buffer. They were basically the corporate embodiment of moral hazard, enjoying the upside of their risk taking while taking comfort that taxpayers would cover any downside. They did not cause the crisis, as some critics have suggested; until late in the boom, the underwriting for mortgages they bought and backed was relatively conservative for the industry. But they did relax their standards before the bust, and by guaranteeing so much mortgage debt in the first place, they did help facilitate the tsunami of foreign money into U.S. real estate that set the stage for the crisis.

All three of us, like our predecessors, had been deeply concerned about Fannie Mae and Freddie Mac for years; we had all supported sweeping reforms of their business model and stricter regulation of their risk taking. The CEOs of both companies had agreed to raise more equity when Hank had called them during the heat of Bear weekend, but only Fannie Mae had raised any, and not nearly enough. Shortly after Bear collapsed, Hank had taken the CEOs to meet Senate Banking Committee chairman Christopher Dodd and ranking Republican Richard Shelby, who had reached an agreement to try to jump-start the House-passed reforms in the Senate, but the legislative process wasn't moving as fast as the markets. By the summer, our top priority was stabilizing the two GSEs before they dragged down the entire system; trillions of dollars' worth of their securities were coursing through the financial bloodstream, and we were afraid they could poison it. Their paper had been considered a safe investment around the world, and now we were fielding calls from nervous officials from sovereign wealth funds and foreign governments who wanted to make sure the GSEs themselves were safe. Some of them hadn't even realized the U.S. government didn't officially backstop Fannie Mae and Freddie Mac.

So Hank decided to ask Congress for the authority to stabilize both mortgage giants, to make explicit the long-standing implicit guarantee that Washington would stand behind the two firms. As with Lehman, he was worried that merely asking for extraordinary powers could confirm how dire the situation was and accelerate the panic. There was a related catch-22: The vast financial authority the Treasury would need to provide a credible backstop for these behemoths seemed politically unrealistic, while requesting an inadequate amount of money could raise doubts about the government's commitment to keeping them afloat. But we all agreed we couldn't stand by and risk a default. So rather than ask for a specific dollar amount, Hank asked for unlimited—his euphemism was "unspecified"—authority to inject capital into Fannie Mae and Freddie Mac. His bill also included some of the reforms he had pushed before the crisis, including a stronger regulator with the power to force Fannie Mae and Freddie Mac into receivership. Ben told Hank he'd support the Treasury 100 percent, just as Hank had supported the Fed in the earlier rescues.

Hank and Ben testified before the Senate committee on July 15, presenting a united front about the importance of the proposed legislation to keep mortgage credit flowing, prevent further deterioration of the housing market, and protect the financial core. Hank's request for a blank check was greeted with skepticism, but he argued that if Congress gave him broad power, the market's anxieties about Fannie Mae and Freddie Mac would dissipate and he'd be less likely to have to use that power. "If you want to make sure it's used, make it small enough and it'll be a self-fulfilling prophecy," he said. "If you've got a squirt gun in your pocket, you may have to take it out. If you've got a bazooka, and people know you've got it, you may not have to take it out." The deterrence argument made sense, but Hank's request for overwhelming firepower revealed concern that panic-riven markets were unlikely to ignore—and he soon knew he might ultimately have to use the bazooka.

Hank was making a remarkably ambitious ask on behalf of a lame-duck president with a 30 percent approval rating. Senator Bunning thundered that the Bear rescue had been "amateur socialism compared to this." And the politics of housing had been tough even before Fannie Mae and Freddie Mac ran off the rails, complicating a spirited debate in Washington about what if anything to do about the rising tide of foreclosures. Some of the public and most congressional Republicans opposed using tax dollars paid by renters and home owners who were making their mortgage payments to provide relief for home owners who weren't. But some of the public and most congressional Democrats felt just as strongly that the government wasn't doing enough to help home owners in trouble. In fact, a fairly inconsequential mortgage relief provision that Barney Frank had inserted in the Fannie Mae–Freddie Mac legislation was even more contentious on Capitol Hill than Hank's request for the fiscal bazooka, so much so that President Bush would forgo a public bill signing when the legislation passed.

But the legislation did pass. Personal relationships matter, and Hank had solid ones with congressional leaders in both parties; most of them agreed to put the emergency ahead of politics. By the end of July, the Democratic-controlled Congress approved the Housing and Economic Recovery Act of 2008 and gave immense power to a Republican administration, proving Washington was capable of doing courageous things when a crisis demanded it, though perhaps no earlier than that.

The new legislation also gave the Treasury and the Fed a chance to look under the hood of Fannie Mae and Freddie Mac, uncovering some ugly surprises. Fed and OCC examiners concluded that both firms were functionally insolvent, with flimsy capital cushions that were mostly accounting fictions. Hank and his team at Treasury soon decided the only solution was to persuade their new regulator, the Federal Housing Finance Agency, to force Fannie Mae and Freddie Mac into conservatorship—basically nationalization without day-to-day government control. It was an awkward situation: He had just told Congress he wouldn't need to use his bazooka, and the FHFA had just told Fannie Mae and Freddie Mac their capital cushions were adequate. But they weren't adequate, and Hank's top priority was avoiding a collapse, not protecting his reputation for consistency. And when Hank concluded he needed to unholster his bazooka after all, President Bush backed him: "It won't always look good, but we are going to do what we need to do to save the economy."

This whatever-it-takes attitude drove almost everything we did during the crisis. We all felt these extraordinary times justified extraordinary actions. Hank brought in two of his former Goldman colleagues and a New York law firm to work on Fannie Mae and Freddie Mac in August. He also leaned hard on the FHFA, pressuring the regulator to reverse its assessment in ways he never would have dreamed of doing before or after the crisis. Hank wasn't even sure he had the legal power to have the government provide the necessary long-term guarantee for the thirty-year mortgages that Fannie Mae and Freddie Mac insured, since Congress had given Treasury only temporary authority, which would expire at the end of 2009. With the help of advisers from Morgan Stanley, Treasury did some clever financial engineering to create what was in effect a long-term guarantee, but Hank was so concerned he might be overstepping congressional intent that he confided to the president and a few of his Treasury colleagues that he was worried he might be impeached. Ultimately, everybody was so shocked when Hank fired his bazooka that nobody even raised that particular question.

On September 5, Hank and Ben gave the CEOs of Fannie Mae and Freddie Mac the stunning news that the government was seizing control of their companies. They would lose their jobs, their shareholders would lose almost all their equity, and the Treasury would inject $100 billion into each company to avoid looming defaults on their debt and the mortgage-backed securities they guaranteed. It was the most aggressive federal intervention in financial markets since the Depression, and the run on Fannie Mae and Freddie Mac quickly subsided, because the companies and the mortgages they insured now had official government backing.

But the run on the rest of the system only gained momentum. The week after the nationalization of Fannie Mae and Freddie Mac saw the worst financial bloodbath since the crisis began. We had hoped that demonstrating the government's willingness to take extraordinary actions to prevent chaotic failures would calm the markets and at least buy us time to cobble together a solution for Lehman Brothers. But once again, our show of force did not have the effect we intended. Markets didn't breathe a sigh of relief; they concluded that if the government was worried enough to take such extraordinary measures, the situation must be even worse than it looked. Uncertainty drives fear, and nobody felt certain what would happen to troubled private firms that didn't have unique federal charters. We weren't certain, either. We had crossed an even bigger Rubicon and averted an even more dangerous panic, but within days, we'd have a still bigger and more dangerous problem on our hands.

CHAPTER FOUR

THE INFERNO:

September 2008–October 2008

THE FIRE BURNED FOR MORE THAN A YEAR BEFORE IT CON- sumed Lehman Brothers, but many Americans still believe the financial crisis began with Lehman's collapse. It eclipsed all that came before and seemed responsible for all that followed. But it was more of a symptom than a cause of the weaknesses in the system; Fannie Mae, Freddie Mac, AIG, and Merrill Lynch were all much larger than Lehman, and all arrived at the brink of collapse around the same time. In fact, Lehman exemplified the factors from which the crisis stemmed. It was a loosely regulated, heavily overleveraged, deeply interconnected nonbank, with too much exposure to the real estate market and too much dangerously runnable short-term financing. What made the story of Lehman different was that it ended in a disaster. Its demise was the most consequential moment of the crisis, and probably the least understood.

Lehman was the nightmare we had been trying to prevent for a year, an uncontrolled failure of a systemically important financial institution during a panic. Since we had saved Bear Stearns in similar circumstances six months earlier, we had just saved Fannie Mae and Freddie Mac a week earlier, and we would go on to save AIG two days later, many observers assumed we had let Lehman fail on purpose—and quite a few praised us for doing so. But we did not let Lehman fail on purpose. We didn't even discuss whether or not to try to save Lehman, as we had with Bear and would with AIG; we knew we had to do everything in our power to try to prevent its collapse. But everything in our power turned out to be insufficient.

In the end, Lehman did not have a buyer that was willing and able to stand behind its obligations, as Bear had with JPMorgan. There was no congressional authorization for the government to stand behind Lehman, as there was for Fannie and Freddie. And Lehman did not have enough solid collateral the Fed could lend against to keep it afloat in a structure the market would accept, as AIG did with its insurance businesses. We helped contribute to the confusion about our motives with some statements we made after Lehman's collapse, when we did not want to rattle the markets by admitting we had been powerless to save a systemic firm. But we had no practical option to save Lehman without a private buyer. Our mindset had not changed in the six months since our close call with Bear, but neither had our constraints. We could not inject capital into Lehman, guarantee its liabilities, buy its assets, or wind it down in an orderly fashion, so our nightmare scenario came true.

That nightmare scenario finally helped us persuade Congress to give us the authority we needed, which would eventually enable us to put out the fire. But we wish we had been able to avoid the scenario in the first place. The pain of Lehman's failure and its aftermath wouldn't be limited to Lehman's shareholders and executives—including Hank's brother Dick, a senior vice president at the firm—or even its counterparties and creditors in the financial system. It would be felt throughout the global economy.

LEHMAN BROTHERS: CIRCLING THE DRAIN

Lehman followed a familiar path to peril, gambling its franchise on subprime mortgage securities, commercial real estate, and other highly leveraged investments that were highly profitable until they weren't. As Lehman's losses mounted and short sellers started betting on its demise, Hank and Tim had pressured its CEO, Dick Fuld, to find a buyer before confidence in his firm completely evaporated. But the terms he was willing to offer potential investors suggested a lack of urgency, and there wasn't much interest in an overextended investment bank, especially when Fuld was still playing hard to get.

On Wednesday, September 10, as Fuld preannounced an ugly third-quarter loss, he tried to blunt the impact by announcing a plan to spin Lehman's toxic assets into a separate company. But that just seemed to confirm the toxicity of the assets he wanted to shed. A reprise of the Bear Stearns endgame was under way: lenders demanding more collateral, hedge funds closing brokerage accounts, ratings agencies threatening downgrades. The markets smelled a corpse, and we feared the fallout; Lehman had more than 100,000 creditors, more than 900,000 open derivatives contracts, and short-term borrowings more than twice those of Bear. It wouldn't go down quietly.

If Lehman had been a commercial bank, the FDIC could have seized it, guaranteed its liabilities, and resolved it to avoid a messy bankruptcy. But no one in the government had the power to do that for a nonbank, so Lehman needed a buyer, just as Bear Stearns had needed a buyer. Bank of America agreed to take a look, but didn't sound serious. Barclays, a U.K.-based bank, expressed more genuine interest, but Fuld, who still thought he could pick and choose his suitor, was skeptical about the fit—and British regulators said they had concerns as well, concerns that would turn out to be consequential. Meanwhile, confidence in several of the other major U.S. firms was eroding rapidly.

We decided to bring Wall Street's top CEOs to the New York Fed on Friday night, September 12, to try to organize a private-sector solution—perhaps something like the Bear deal with Wall Street firms taking on risk instead of the Fed; or together with the Fed, to help another larger and stronger firm acquire Lehman; or perhaps even something like the 1998 deal where the New York Fed encouraged fourteen counterparties of Long-Term Capital Management to band together to buy the firm outright and liquidate its assets. This time, Wall Street had even greater reason to help avoid a collapse. Merrill Lynch looked like it would be the next domino to fall after Lehman, and then Morgan Stanley; not even Goldman Sachs, the investment bank with the strongest balance sheet and largest liquidity cushion, could survive an all-out run on its business model.

Unfortunately, we weren't optimistic that something workable would emerge. Lehman was much bigger than LTCM had been at the time of its collapse, and its assets were much shakier. Meanwhile, the other firms whose cash would be needed for a rescue were much more fragile than they had been in 1998, and they didn't have much capital to spare to keep a competitor from imploding. They had to worry about their own resilience to shocks, because there was no reason to think the shocks would end anytime soon. AIG, the massive insurer that insured many of their securities against default, had lost half its value that week and was besieged by margin calls. An internal New York Fed email warned that even as Lehman circled the drain, Wall Street was just as nervous about AIG: "I am hearing worse than LEH. Every bank and dealer has exposure to them." It was chilling to think how disastrous the situation would have been if Fannie and Freddie had been imploding as well, but the situation was pretty disastrous even after they were nationalized and stabilized.

Meanwhile, Washington was becoming a cauldron of burn-the-arsonists fervor, with politicians from both parties expressing increasing anger at Wall Street bailouts. The broader economy had not yet felt the full effects of the mounting panic—the Fed had not even cut rates in August, as the distress on Wall Street took time to reach Main Street—but there were now signs of extreme strain, with auto sales plunging and layoffs rising sharply. Understandably, Americans were enraged and puzzled by the extraordinary efforts being made to rescue the bankers responsible for the mess. Meanwhile, editorials in the *Financial Times* and *Wall Street Journal* as well as the nonfinancial press were imploring us to stop rewarding failure.

As Lehman entered its endgame, Hank and his team put out the word that taxpayers would not subsidize a Lehman deal. This was a negotiating tactic, not a policy decision. He was trying to motivate the private sector to assume as much of Lehman's bad assets as possible, to increase the likelihood that a Bear Stearns–like rescue would be possible. But this was one of the few moments during the crisis when we were not all on the same page. Tim thought that telling the private sector it was on its own would intensify the run, and he was concerned that a "no government money" proclamation would hurt our credibility if the Fed did get the opportunity to assist a buyer with a Bear Stearns–type loan.

But Hank said he would gladly reverse his position if we got an opportunity to save Lehman. We all knew that if the government needed to take some risk to get Lehman sold through a Bear-type deal, we would do it even if we didn't like it, because a Lehman collapse would be far costlier in terms of financial and economic stability than a Lehman bailout. We were determined to avoid disruptive failures of major institutions until we could draw a circle of protection around the system's core, and at that point we didn't have the power to build that kind of firewall. Our disagreement was about negotiating and messaging tactics, not our ultimate determination to do whatever we could to prevent a destabilizing collapse of a systemic firm.

By the closing bell on Friday, Lehman was down to its last $2 billion in cash, just as Bear had been on its last day. At the New York Fed, Tim and Hank warned the leaders of Wall Street's top firms that a Lehman default would be catastrophic for all of them, so they needed to work together to prevent it.

The New York Fed swarmed all weekend with bankers, lawyers, accountants, and regulators working against the clock to avoid a meltdown. One team met with potential Lehman acquirers to identify the bad assets they wanted to leave behind, while another worked with the consortium of Wall Street banks to encourage them to take on some or all of these bad assets. Everyone who reviewed Lehman's books was appalled. Bank of America told us it wouldn't even consider a deal unless it could leave behind $70 billion in bad assets; Barclays identified $52 billion it wouldn't take. The Wall Street executives analyzing Lehman's real estate portfolio concluded it was only worth about half what the firm claimed. The industry had some incentive to exaggerate the problems to encourage the government to help, but Lehman clearly had a huge capital hole that would have to be filled to complete any deal, posing as much as ten times the risk the Fed had taken with Bear.

That was a daunting hole for a private-sector consortium to try to fill. And the CEOs of stronger firms had a legitimate concern that markets would punish them if it looked like they were now responsible for rescuing failing rivals. What would happen Monday if another consortium was needed to rescue AIG, a firm with tens of millions of life insurance customers and tens of billions of dollars' worth of retirement assets? On Saturday morning, AIG alerted the Fed it might need a $30 billion bridge loan; by evening, the request had skyrocketed to $60 billion.

Still, the news was not all bad that Saturday night: Bank of America was working out a deal to buy Merrill Lynch without government or industry assistance, which helped explain why its executives had shown so little interest in shopping for Lehman.

We were relieved to have one existential threat defused, even though it meant only one potential buyer left for Lehman. And by the end of the night, the Barclays-Lehman merger looked like a real possibility. The Wall Street CEOs had agreed in principle to take on the risk of a big slug of Lehman's distressed assets to help Barclays buy the firm and avoid a damaging default. There were still unanswered questions, and we suspected last-minute Fed assistance might be necessary to close the deal. Barclays CEO Bob Diamond also raised a troubling issue: British law required a shareholder vote before the merger could be finalized, and he wasn't sure his firm would be able to guarantee Lehman's obligations until the deal was done. That would clearly be a problem, but it didn't feel like the kind of problem that would scuttle a deal with Armageddon hanging in the balance. We figured that if the other issues could be resolved, we'd work something out with the British.

We figured wrong. On Sunday morning, British regulators blocked the deal. Callum McCarthy, the U.K.'s top financial regulator, told Tim he wasn't sure Barclays had enough capital to take on Lehman's risk, or enough capacity to guarantee Lehman's troubled assets. He said that in any case, Barclays wouldn't be permitted to backstop Lehman's obligations until its shareholders approved a merger that he didn't sound willing to approve himself, and a shareholder vote could take weeks or even months to arrange. Tim told him the markets needed immediate certainty about Lehman's fate, so delaying the deal was tantamount to killing it at a moment when global financial stability was at stake. McCarthy's response was: "Good luck."

Hank made a last-ditch call to ask U.K. finance minister Alistair Darling to waive the requirement for a shareholder vote, so Barclays could stand behind Lehman right away. But Darling made it clear he didn't intend to help, because he didn't want British taxpayers on the hook for Lehman's problems. As Hank reported to Tim: "He didn't want to import our cancer." The Barclays deal was dead. We were frustrated by the refusal of U.K. regulators to help avoid a cataclysm, but they had some legitimate concerns. Their banking system was four times larger than ours as a percentage of our respective economies, and equally fragile. Importing Lehman's disease to Barclays could have exposed their taxpayers to serious losses if the combined firm ultimately required a government rescue. The British weren't crazy to worry that Barclays would end up like the proverbial drunk who tries to help another drunk out of a ditch but ends up falling into the ditch himself.

As unthinkable as it seemed, we were out of options. We didn't have the authority to fill Lehman's capital hole or guarantee its obligations on our own; all we had was the Fed's power to lend against solid collateral. The Fed did have some discretion about what counted as acceptable collateral, but some of the sharpest minds in government and finance had just reviewed Lehman's assets, and the verdict had been as brutal as the market's. Lehman appeared to be deeply insolvent; a 2013 study would conclude its capital hole might have been as big as $200 billion. And while the Fed would have helped finance an acquisition as it had with Bear, it couldn't rescue an insolvent firm in the midst of a run. Apart from the large losses on Lehman's balance sheet, the market's confidence in the strength of its businesses, its brand, and its management had seriously eroded. We had months of evidence of its inability to raise capital, sell assets, or finance its real estate portfolio at anywhere near its stated value. We were willing to take risks in extremis, but the Fed's tools, limited to lending against collateral, could not make Lehman viable.

Even if the Fed had decided, contrary to the available evidence, that the value of the firm justified lending to Lehman on a massive scale, lending into what had already become an unstoppable run on the firm would only have given some of the firm's remaining creditors and counterparties a chance to flee at taxpayer expense as Lehman's businesses continued inexorably to erode. That kind of bridge loan to nowhere would have created huge losses for the government without quelling the panic, and the backlash might have crippled our ability to act the next time a major institution needed help—which, as it turned out, would be Tuesday. A lender of last resort can help reduce the risk that viable companies go down because of temporary liquidity problems, but it can't make fundamentally nonviable companies viable. If markets believe a firm is irrevocably insolvent, a secured loan cannot stop a run or bring back fleeing customers and counterparties.

At 1:45 a.m. on Monday, September 15, Lehman filed for bankruptcy, the largest in American history. The Fed tried to apply foam on the runway by stating its willingness to lend to banks and investment banks against just about any form of collateral. But the explosion was devastating anyway.

The cost of insuring the bonds of Morgan Stanley and Goldman Sachs doubled on Monday, as markets lost confidence in the investment bank business model. The run also extended into the commercial banking sector. Citi's credit default swaps spiked, reflecting growing market fears that even too-big-to-fail banks might fail, and spooked depositors withdrew twice as much from Washington Mutual as they had withdrawn after the run on Indy-Mac. Even the industrial giant General Electric struggled to roll over its commercial paper, a troubling sign that the financial virus had infected the broader economy. Banks, businesses, and households around the world retreated into a defensive shell; pension and retirement funds plummeted in value; and the vicious cycle of foreclosures, layoffs, and financial panic intensified. Foreign banks that had borrowed from U.S. money market funds and U.S. banks lost access to dollars, and emerging markets were also deprived of financial oxygen. The Fed substantially expanded its swap lines to provide dollars to foreign central banks, and generally provided markets in the United States and abroad with unprecedented liquidity during an unprecedented liquidity crunch. But the Fed's short-term lending could not by itself fix a global crisis of confidence.

After Lehman failed, editorialists in the *New York Times*, the *Wall Street Journal*, and other influential outlets were pleased that we had resisted the temptation to use public dollars to rescue a failed enterprise. For a brief moment, critics who had vilified us as bailout kings hailed our commitment to free-market discipline, our willingness to teach Wall Street a lesson by letting irresponsible speculators pay for their sins. But the praise was misguided, as was the scattered criticism that we were idiots to let Lehman fail. We would have rescued Lehman if we could have. Yes, Hank had suggested before Lehman went down that the government wouldn't help, but that was a tactic to pressure the private sector to participate in a rescue that the Fed and the Treasury lacked the power to execute on their own. In the days following the collapse, Hank and Ben also noted in congressional testimony that the markets had time to prepare for Lehman's failure, which gave some critics the impression that we had expected the resulting damage to be modest. But we had agreed among ourselves that at least for the moment, we needed to downplay our inability to save Lehman, because we feared that such an admission would terrify the markets and accelerate the run. Public communication during a panic is both vitally important and incredibly difficult, and we were trying to find a balance between being blunt and being reassuring. We did help feed the myth that we chose failure, to avoid confessing publicly that we were out of ammunition, but in reality, we just weren't able to prevent failure.

The fall of Lehman dramatically accelerated the crisis, but a less frantic, less visible run on the financial system had been building for more than a year. In an analogy coined by the economist Edward Lazear, Lehman was the first major kernel of popcorn we couldn't prevent from popping, but it didn't create the heat in the pan. And even if we had somehow saved Lehman, we would have lacked the authority to turn down the heat to prevent other kernels from popping. We were in another catch-22 situation: We needed substantial new authorities, including the ability to put capital into teetering financial firms, to stop the crisis. But we never could have gotten that authority from Congress without a spectacular failure like Lehman. And even then it would be a struggle. We did not choose to let Lehman fail, but even if we had somehow found a solution for that firm, something else was eventually going to break.

We had stretched our authority to its limits, but the limits were real, and it was now painfully clear that we couldn't put out the fire until we could deploy the full resources of the U.S. government. That Sunday night after Lehman's fate was sealed, we all agreed it was time to go to Congress to get the money and tools we needed. First, though, we had to deal with AIG, which was even bigger and more dangerous than Lehman, and was threatening to burn down what was left of the system.

AIG: FREE MARKET DAY

Like Lehman, the global insurer AIG had fallen through the cracks of our broken regulatory system. Its insurance subsidiaries were regulated at the state level, while the Office of Thrift Supervision, the light-touch regulator of choice for institutions like Countrywide, IndyMac, and WaMu, purported to oversee its holding company. None of us had visibility into AIG, and none of us had paid close attention to the firm until it started to hemorrhage late that summer. But the more we learned about the company, the more we realized that letting it follow Lehman's path would be a recipe for a depression.

AIG insured the lives, health, property, vehicles, and retirement accounts of 76 million customers, including 180,000 businesses that employed more than two thirds of the American workforce. And thanks to its irresponsible Financial Products division, which resembled a hedge fund grafted on to a traditional insurance company, AIG also had $2.7 trillion worth of derivatives contracts, mostly credit default swaps insuring troubled financial instruments. If it collapsed, the other systemic banks and nonbanks would lose their disaster insurance when they needed it most. It seemed like everyone was exposed to AIG, and no one was sure how exposed anyone else was, so an AIG default could inspire runs on just about any other financial firm.

Now that default seemed imminent. AIG's stock plunged below $5 on Monday, down from more than $150 at its peak; its counterparties were demanding huge amounts of additional collateral; and the ratings agencies were considering a crippling downgrade. It now looked like AIG needed at least $75 billion to stay afloat, the kind of hole only the government could fill at a time when banks were hoarding liquidity. We had never imagined that the Fed should help an insurer, and just a few days earlier, we had doubted we could. But by Monday afternoon, it was clear that AIG was too big, too complex, and too broken to be rescued by the private sector, and that the system was in no shape to handle its collapse.

As with Lehman, we didn't have a mechanism like the FDIC's bank resolution authority that we could use to wind down AIG without bankruptcy and default, and we couldn't inject capital, guarantee liabilities, or buy assets. This time, though, we did think the Fed might be able to lend to AIG in amounts sufficient to stave off its collapse. Unlike investment banks, which have nothing if they don't have trust and confidence, AIG had a global empire of relatively stable income-generating insurance businesses. The Fed had the authority to lend against good collateral, and unlike Bear or Lehman, AIG had a collection of regulated insurance subsidiaries with premium-paying policyholders and mandatory reserves that it could use to back its loans. The markets had lost confidence in AIG's ability to survive a run on its funding, but its problems were primarily in its holding company, which housed its beleaguered Financial Products division. We thought the markets would recognize that its valuable insurance operations were sufficient to keep the enterprise fundamentally solvent and viable.

Any loan to a failing company in the throes of a run would still be risky, and we knew it might only buy the system time to prepare for a default. But by Tuesday, AIG was about to file for bankruptcy if it didn't get the cash it needed, and the amount of cash it needed seemed to increase every hour. That afternoon, the Fed sent AIG a take-it-or-leave-it offer of an $85 billion credit line at a penalty interest rate in exchange for 79.9 percent of the firm—just below the threshold that would force the government to bring the company formally onto its balance sheet, but enough to ensure taxpayers would get most of the upside if the firm survived. AIG accepted the deal, even though one condition was that we would immediately replace its CEO.

We knew the backlash would be intense, and we knew it would look like we were lurching. Barney Frank quipped that September 15 should be dubbed Free Market Day, in honor of America's one-day commitment to market rigor between Lehman and AIG. But we didn't suddenly embrace or abandon any principles. We did what we could do to prevent chaos and we didn't do what we couldn't do; AIG had solid collateral, enough to secure the funding it needed to stay in business, while Lehman didn't. And even with AIG, we tried to drive a tough bargain, partly to maximize the protection for taxpayers, partly to minimize the moral hazard we'd create for the future. AIG's shareholders later sued because they thought they were treated too harshly, and as galling as that was, it did reflect our commitment to saving the broader system rather than everyone in it. Rescuing AIG was our least awful option at the time, and we tried to minimize its awfulness.

Critics mocked us for sending Wall Street another message that failure would be rewarded. But most of the failures hadn't been rewarded. Over the course of the crisis, the CEOs of Countrywide, Bear, Fannie, Freddie, Merrill, Lehman, AIG, Citi, and

Wachovia had all lost their jobs. The shareholders of every financial firm had seen their stock prices plunge. It's true that we had reduced some pain in the financial sector to avoid an all-out stampede by creditors and counterparties, which presumably created some moral hazard. But we weren't creating a particularly inviting path for future financiers to follow, and it would have been a bizarre act of hubris for us to let the financial system implode and drag down the economy just so we could feel righteous about the stern precedent we had set. We would have gladly let AIG fail if we thought the fallout could be limited to the company's executives and shareholders, but we did not want any systemically dangerous institution to fail at a time when we had no way to prevent the damage from escalating into a global catastrophe.

Some critics were outraged that the Fed didn't insist on haircuts that would have reduced the payouts to AIG's creditors and counterparties, which instead received 100 cents on the dollar for their risky arrangements with a dying firm. In fact, the Fed didn't have the power to impose haircuts without triggering a default that would mean certain bankruptcy, and the creditors quickly rejected the idea of accepting even minuscule haircuts voluntarily. In any case, while haircuts for creditors of unraveling firms are sensible and just in normal times—and a common feature of the normal bankruptcy process—haircuts during a panic are a sure way to make the panic worse. They send a signal to creditors of other troubled firms that they're also risking a haircut if they don't run immediately, a phenomenon we would witness just a week later with Washington Mutual. The goal of crisis response should be to alleviate fears, not to confirm and amplify them.

We understood why the public wanted to see financial firms pay the ultimate price for their recklessness. As the saying goes, capitalism without bankruptcy is like Christianity without hell. But policymakers who focus on retribution rather than stabilization during an epic crisis will only make the crisis more epic. As Ben has put it, if your neighbor sets his house on fire by smoking in bed, you want the fire department to put it out before it spreads to your house and your entire town, even though letting it burn would punish the perpetrator and send a strong message that smoking in bed will never be tolerated. It makes sense to try to avoid rewarding the reckless beyond what's needed to contain the fire, and to punish them appropriately (while promoting stronger fire prevention measures) after the fire is out. But the first priority has to be putting the fire out.

It turned out that AIG was in even more dire straits than we thought. It would continue to unravel after its initial loan, and the rescue would end up expanding to an unthinkable $185 billion. Eventually, though, AIG would pay the money back with interest, in part by selling off operations, and the government would make a $23 billion profit. More important, we avoided the broader damage that would have followed AIG's default. The company's executives had helped put the entire system at risk, which made the public even more furious when they received bonuses that had been contracted before the crisis. From a public relations perspective, saving AIG was devastating. But in September 2008, on the day after Lehman's failure, failing to save AIG would have been calamitous.

THE END OF AN ERA

We had averted quite a few disasters, but that was not enough. Lehman's failure and the near-failure of Merrill and AIG helped send markets into even deeper shock. The two surviving stand-alone investment banks both faced intensifying runs; Morgan Stanley's credit default swaps spiked higher than Lehman's had before it failed, while Goldman Sachs watched $60 billion worth of liquidity evaporate in a week. Corporate bond spreads widened twice as much as they had after the crash of 1929, suggesting fears of widespread bankruptcies among nonfinancial firms. Yields on short-term Treasury bills actually went negative, reflecting the frenetic flight to safety; investors were so afraid of investing in anything that they were willing to pay the government to hold their cash. Ben got an email from the baseball statistics guru Bill James urging him to hang in there: "At some point the people who are saying it can't get any worse HAVE to be right."

It was still getting worse, and a new disaster erupted on Tuesday while we were finalizing the terms of our support for AIG. The Reserve Primary Fund, a money market fund that had invested heavily in Lehman's commercial paper, announced it could no longer pay its investors 100 cents on the dollar and was halting redemptions. Investors afraid that other money market funds would also "break the buck" and freeze their cash scrambled to pull $230 billion out of the industry that week, a scary run on quasi-banks that had operated without insurance for their quasi-deposits. Meanwhile, as money funds pulled back from risk to reassure their investors, they bought even less commercial paper and lent even less in the repo markets, intensifying the liquidity crisis for banks and nonbanks. CEOs of highly rated nonfinancial companies like General Electric, Ford, and even Coca-Cola warned Hank that they were having trouble selling their paper, depriving them of the short-term funding they relied on to manage operations and pay their suppliers and workers. That would force them to cut back inventories and delay payments to small and midsize suppliers, which would in turn be forced to lay off workers.

The crisis was about to spread, in a more concrete and palpable way, from Wall Street to Main Street. We were determined to stop the runs on money market funds, which invested $3.5 trillion for 30 million Americans, and commercial paper, which provided vital day-to-day liquidity that was the lifeblood of so many real-economy companies. Hank's team came up with the idea of using Treasury's $50 billion Exchange Stabilization Fund to guarantee the money funds just as the FDIC guaranteed bank deposits. The Treasury fund was supposed to be used to protect the value of the dollar only in an emergency, but there was a case to be made that stopping runs on money funds would prevent an economic collapse that could destroy the value of the dollar. Anyway, we believed that once Treasury announced the guarantee, it wouldn't have to spend or lend anything, because investors would stop running once they regained confidence the money funds were safe. And the Fed buttressed the new guarantee by launching a new entry in its alphabet soup of lending programs, the AMLF (Asset-Backed Commercial Paper Money Market Mutual Fund Liquidity Facility), a circuitous effort to thaw the market for asset-backed commercial paper by helping banks buy it from money funds. Within two weeks, the program was financing $150 billion worth of securities the market no longer trusted.

The interventions worked. No other money market funds broke the buck, and since Treasury charged them all a premium for their new insurance policy, taxpayers ended up turning another profit. The extra liquidity from the Fed helped, but the real lesson was the power of a government guarantee; when crisis managers can credibly promise protection against catastrophic outcomes, market participants don't have to act in anticipation of those outcomes, so the feared outcomes don't happen.

We had no authority to guarantee the liabilities of investment banks, so we spent some long hours pushing Morgan Stanley CEO John Mack and Goldman's Lloyd Blankfein to seek mergers with commercial banks that had stronger funding bases. At this point Tim had tried to arrange so many shotgun marriages that Wall Street executives were calling him "eharmony." But potential megamergers like Goldman–Wachovia and Morgan–Citi didn't really make sense; Wachovia and Citi had their own challenges despite their insured deposits, and the matches raised two-drunks-in-a-ditch concerns. Meanwhile, we reluctantly encouraged the SEC to impose a temporary ban on the short selling of shares of financial firms, something we had resisted for months, and never would have considered in less extreme circumstances.

We hated the idea of prohibiting bets against companies in trouble—it felt like outlawing negative reviews, which could undermine confidence in the marketplace we wanted to protect—but Morgan Stanley was on the brink of collapse, and Goldman would have followed, with major commercial banks close behind. Then we wouldn't have had much left to protect.

Both investment banks were desperately looking for strategic partners to make cornerstone equity investments that would help bolster their capital cushions and send a signal of confidence in the viability of their businesses. The Fed decided to allow both to become bank holding companies, but only on the condition that they raise significant private capital right away. Over the weekend of September 20, Goldman Sachs worked to secure a $5 billion investment from Warren Buffett, which enabled the firm to raise another $5 billion from the public. And Morgan Stanley secured a commitment from Mitsubishi to buy 20 percent of the firm for $9 billion. The bank holding company designation by the Fed was vaguely reassuring to the market, but in reality it had few substantive implications. For example, given the lending programs already in place, it didn't increase how much either investment bank could borrow from the Fed.

The capital injections by private investors provided a limited vote of confidence, but the financial fire was still raging. We were dangerously behind the curve of the panic, and our existing arsenal of tools had proven to be too weak to contain the force of the run. We needed a way to forestall disasters for the entire financial sector, rather than stepping in one firm at a time, and there would be no way to do that without congressional buy-in and taxpayer dollars.

For months, we had wanted to ask for stronger emergency authorities, but Congress had signaled it would need more compelling evidence that we really needed more power, and we had feared that a conspicuous public rejection would intensify market concerns about our ability to end the crisis. But now we were staring into the abyss of a second depression, and for the first time we believed we might be able to get a reluctant Congress to act. In a meeting in the Roosevelt Room of the White House on September 18, Ben and Hank told President Bush that the time had come to go to Congress; Ben emphasized that there was nothing more the Fed could do on its own. So the president gave us the go-ahead to go to Capitol Hill to ask for the firepower we needed, so we could make sure there would be no more Lehman-style failures.

Late that Friday night, Hank sent Congress a three-page draft of a Troubled Assets Relief Program, a proposal to give Treasury the power to buy $700 billion worth of the toxic mortgage securities that had poisoned the financial system. The dollar figure was somewhat arbitrary—$500 billion didn't feel quite large enough relative to the $11 trillion residential mortgage market, while anything closer to $1 trillion felt too large for the political system to swallow—but the goal was to create the perception and the reality of overwhelming force. We hoped to bolster confidence in endangered financial firms by removing some of the illiquid assets weighing down their balance sheets; we also hoped the purchases would revive the market for similar mortgage assets that we didn't buy, effectively recapitalizing the entire financial system. This was similar to a so-called break-the-glass plan that Treasury and the Fed had developed jointly in April, and it was clearly time to break the glass.

The mere act of publicly advocating for TARP carried some risk. Hank and Ben needed to convince Congress the situation was dire enough to justify extraordinary action, but excessively alarmist rhetoric could end up inflaming the panic; it was the same communications tightrope we had walked throughout the crisis. And Hank's bare-bones proposal created an immediate political firestorm of its own. It was intended as a mere outline, a response to Senator Dodd's request that he not present Congress a fait accompli, but critics mocked its lack of legislative details.

The draft also included virtually unlimited flexibility for Treasury to spend $700 billion without congressional interference or even judicial review, prompting accusations that Hank was seeking unprecedented power. Many Republicans attacked the plan as big-government socialism, while many Democrats complained that it lacked restrictions on executive compensation and relief for home owners. At a series of hearings on Capitol Hill, Hank and Ben were repeatedly pilloried for putting Wall Street ahead of Main Street, for coddling arsonists rather than letting them burn. One senator told Ben that calls to his office about the proposed legislation were running "50 percent no, 50 percent hell no."

Still, away from the cameras and the congressional posturing, Hank was making progress toward a bipartisan deal when Senator John McCain, the Republican presidential nominee, suddenly announced he was suspending his campaign and flying back to Washington to help resolve the crisis, thrusting the negotiations into the whirlwind of presidential politics. Hank warned McCain that if he torpedoed TARP, Hank would publicly say that he was sabotaging the economy, which, of course, he did not want to have to do. He even suggested that Ben might support him, which was not in fact something Ben would have done as an independent Fed chair, but Hank was willing to bluff a bit to avert a catastrophe.

President Bush and Hank met at the White House that Thursday, September 25, with presidential candidates McCain and Obama and congressional leaders of both parties, a famously unproductive meeting that ended in a raucous shouting match after key Republicans remained resistant to TARP. The politics of financial crises are always difficult, even when they don't erupt before presidential elections, because the actions necessary to stabilize financial systems are never popular. This is why it's so vital for crisis managers to have the tools they need before a crisis, so that they don't need to rely on political leaders to take political risks in real time under the public microscope. As Tim's aide Lee Sachs pointed out, a fire department shouldn't have to call a town meeting to approve the purchase of new equipment to fight a fire that's already burning out of control.

In fact, on that same Thursday the fire burned down another huge firm, Washington Mutual, which overtook IndyMac as the largest FDIC-insured bank ever to fail. FDIC chair Sheila Bair worked out a deal for JPMorgan Chase to buy WaMu and protect its deposits without assistance from her agency's insurance fund. But the FDIC's deal not only wiped out WaMu's shareholders, which was appropriate, it imposed heavy losses on WaMu's senior debt holders. In other words, it allowed WaMu to default on its debt obligations, the result we had been so desperate to avoid for other firms. This kind of haircut makes sense in ordinary times, forcing creditors to suffer the consequences of their unwise loans, but not during panics, when it sends a message that creditors of other financial firms should run. Bair thought our rescues had created too much moral hazard, and saw WaMu's failure as a teachable moment for the financial system. She was also very protective of the FDIC's Deposit Insurance Fund, often citing her legal obligation to seek the least-cost option for her agency. But there was a "systemic risk exception" to that obligation when financial stability was at stake, and haircutting WaMu seemed like it would create significant risk of more bank failures, more FDIC losses, more rescues, and more moral hazard.

Sure enough, the next morning there was a run on Wachovia, the next domino in line, and the fourth-largest bank in the country by assets. The cost of insuring Wachovia's senior debt against default doubled, and the price of its ten-year bonds dropped by nearly two thirds in one day. Once again, we needed a weekend solution for a collapsing megabank, and while Citigroup and Wells Fargo were both interested, neither was willing to buy Wachovia and stand behind its obligations without government help. Initially, Bair was inclined to rerun her WaMu playbook of haircutting senior creditors to protect the FDIC fund and avoid moral hazard. But after some debate, she agreed to invoke the systemic risk exception to avoid another chaotic default that would have ramped up the panic.

That didn't quite end the drama over Wachovia. The FDIC initially announced a sale to Citi, while agreeing to take some of the risk of Wachovia's bad mortgage assets, but changed its mind when Wells Fargo made a new offer that required neither haircuts nor FDIC help. This was an understandable reversal, but the government's zigzags were creating all kinds of uncertainty in the markets. The appearance of lurching without a coherent strategy was mostly the consequence of the government's limited powers, fragmented authorities, and the general messiness of financial crises. But it didn't exactly bolster confidence that we had a handle on the situation, and this limited the effectiveness of the tools we did have.

We wanted to assure the markets there would be no more Lehmans or WaMus, and to make those assurances credible we needed TARP. Over Wachovia weekend, Hank and his team hashed out a deal with congressional leaders that added oversight measures to his minimalist draft, as well as restrictions on golden parachutes for CEOs at participating institutions. Hank had resisted a stricter crackdown on executive compensation in order to limit the stigma associated with TARP, because it wouldn't work unless banks agreed to participate even if they weren't on the brink of failure. Still, his first priority was a deal, and Treasury got everything Hank thought he needed in the deal. And McCain and Obama both showed political courage by supporting it.

Nevertheless, on Monday, September 29, the House narrowly rejected the TARP bill. The S&P 500 dropped 9 percent, wiping out a record $1 trillion in value. It was a deeply frightening moment, jolting some recalcitrant House Republicans to their senses. After Senate leaders added some tax breaks to TARP, they passed the bill on Wednesday with broad bipartisan support. And on Friday, the House did an about-face and passed the sweetened version as well. It hadn't been pretty, but during a national emergency, a Democratic-controlled Congress (with some Republican support) had passed a politically radioactive $700 billion Wall Street rescue for a Republican administration in just sixteen days. The bill gave Treasury remarkably expansive power, making it clear that Hank didn't even have to use the Troubled Assets Relief Program to buy troubled assets. Barney Frank joked that he could use it to buy gravel if he wanted. That was not Hank's plan, but by the time the bill passed, the Treasury and the Fed were focusing on a different alternative to buying troubled assets.

CHAPTER FIVE

DOUSING THE FIRE:

October 2008–May 2009

THE PASSAGE OF TARP WAS A TURNING POINT, THE MOMENT when the democratically elected branches of government officially recognized that the crisis posed a grave threat to the economy and gave crisis managers expanded authority to stabilize the financial system. But the system remained unstable for quite a while.

Part of the problem was simply that the system was in such bad shape. It had been taking hits for fourteen months, and the chaos of September—not only the collapse of Lehman but the near-failures of Fannie Mae and Freddie Mac, Merrill Lynch, and AIG, along with the unprecedented run on money market funds—had been a devastating blow to credit markets and confidence. The approval of $700 billion worth of assistance was welcome news, but the system had more than $700 billion worth of problems, and fear was building about the solvency of other significant financial firms. In fact, the spread reflecting stress in interbank lending hit an all-time high during the week *after* Congress enacted TARP; the stock market had its worst week since 1933. Clearly, the mere existence of TARP wasn't going to quell the panic. We needed to announce a clear plan to settle the markets immediately, and we needed to implement it quickly.

Unfortunately, the no-confidence virus that had infected mortgage securities, firms exposed to mortgage securities, and firms exposed to the exposed firms had also spread to the Fed and the Treasury. We were supposed to make things better, yet things kept getting worse, and markets were increasingly skeptical that we could control the contagion. They wanted to see a consistent and forceful strategy they could rely on, but the constraints on our authority had contributed to a sense that we were making it up as we went along, saving some firms but not others, falling behind the curve of the crisis. And now that Congress had finally expanded our authority with TARP Hank decided not to use it to buy troubled assets. It looked like we were improvising again, but in a crisis, it's vital to have the courage to change course when the times demand it.

One reason the fire still looked so ominous despite our upgraded firefighting equipment was the worsening state of the broader economy. It had slipped into recession the previous December, but the turmoil of the fall had accelerated the doom loop between the financial sector and the real economy: job losses and loan defaults, further sapping confidence and depressing asset prices, leading to more belt-tightening, layoffs, defaults, and fire sales, deepening the financial crisis as well as the economic downturn. As the economy imploded, it became increasingly rational to assume the worst about struggling U.S. financial firms. And the situation was at least as bad in Europe, where seven different nations had to step in to nationalize one or more failing institutions.

Still, now that we had TARP, we felt like we could finally get ahead of the curve.

DEPLOYING TARP

When we first proposed TARP, Hank believed asset purchases would be a better mechanism for restoring financial stability than capital investments. His goal was to recapitalize the banking system. But in the past, whenever governments had injected capital directly into private banks, the terms had often been so punitive that only failed or failing banks had accepted the capital, resulting in expensive nationalization of the weakest banks without much recapitalization of the entire system. Hank believed that buying distressed assets would boost the prices of assets remaining in the banks, strengthening their balance sheets, improving their capital positions, and shoring up investor confidence. By contrast, capital injections raised the specter of nationalization, which risked accelerating the flight from the major banks. In recent weeks, shareholders in Fannie Mae, Freddie Mac, and AIG had been nearly wiped out after the government had taken equity stakes in those enterprises, and Hank feared that other bank shareholders would flee if they thought their equity was at risk of getting diluted as well. He was also concerned about the political reaction to what might look like a partial nationalization of the financial system.

While we were seeking emergency powers from Congress, we had to deal with the two largest bank failures in U.S. history, Washington Mutual and Wachovia, and by the time TARP was enacted, the situation was deteriorating at an alarming rate. We needed immediate action to settle the markets. And it quickly became clear that designing a fair and effective program of asset purchases would be a complex and difficult task. The bottom line was that the system needed more capital, and buying assets was an indirect and inefficient way to boost capital levels; there was also no easy way to determine which assets Treasury should buy and how much it should pay. Hank's team considered various approaches involving auctions and partnerships with private-sector investors, but it was clear that setting up a workable program would take six weeks or longer. We would revisit some of these ideas in the coming months, but we needed a simpler, swifter, and more efficient approach to get help to the system while there was still a system to help.

By the time Congress approved TARP, we all agreed that injecting capital directly into financial institutions by having the government buy their newly issued stock would be a much easier and quicker way to stabilize the banking system than by buying their assets. It would also be much more powerful and cost effective. We needed to stretch every TARP dollar as far as we could; $700 billion was a lot of money, but we were worried that asset purchases could blow through all of it without resolving the underlying problems. Hank's team also decided to buy nonvoting preferred stock rather than common equity, which would help calm fears of a government takeover, and to do so on relatively attractive terms, so that strong as well as weak banks would accept the capital and restore confidence in the system.

For fourteen months, our powers had been limited to the Fed's efforts to address liquidity problems; now government capital could finally address the underlying solvency problems. But with the panic building, banks still struggling to finance themselves, and the magnitude of the potential losses increasing, we feared that capital injections alone would be insufficient to stabilize the system. Creditors and investors were still pulling back from strong as well as weak financial firms. The simplest and most powerful way to ensure that banks could attract financing was to guarantee their debts, just as Treasury had done for money market funds after the Reserve Primary Fund broke the buck. We wanted to make a credible commitment that there would be no more haircuts or defaults, because that's how confidence gets restored and runs are stopped, and we had seen with the money funds that the markets considered federal guarantees to be credible. Several European countries had already decided to provide comprehensive guarantees for their bank liabilities, so our defenses would have to be similarly comprehensive.

It occurred to us that since the FDIC did have the power to backstop failing banks one at a time, it could invoke its systemic risk exception to backstop all banks at once. FDIC chair Sheila Bair was reluctant to expose her agency's Deposit Insurance Fund to more risk, and had criticized our whatever-it-takes approach to protecting systemic institutions as overly generous to Wall Street. But she had seen the chaotic market reactions to the defaults by Lehman and WaMu, and to her credit, she agreed to consider guaranteeing some bank obligations.

Initially, Bair pushed to limit the guarantees—by restricting them to newly issued debt, excluding the debts of bank holding companies, imposing punitive fees on banks that used the guarantees, and even limiting the guarantees to 90 percent of the debts, an implicit 10 percent haircut. She argued that she had only $35 billion in her insurance fund, so she had to be careful about risk. But we argued that taking some risk up front to protect banks against runs would reduce the risk that cascading failures would drain her entire fund. And she had the ability to borrow from the Treasury to backstop her fund; the FDIC could also increase fees on the financial industry to replenish its fund after the crisis was over.

We wanted to throw everything we had at the crisis, so even as we raced to hash out the details of the government capital and guarantees, we were launching additional efforts to protect the system. The Fed set up a new lending program to prevent the collapse of the commercial paper market, so major corporations could finance their operations for longer than a day or two. The Commercial Paper Funding Facility (CPFF) involved another novel interpretation of the Fed's emergency authority, but it would buy $242 billion worth of paper in its first week, helping to unclog important short-term credit channels for businesses. And the program would end up earning $849 million for taxpayers, never incurring a single loss.

At the same time, with an unprecedented chill spreading through the global economy, we announced some unprecedented actions with our global counterparts. First, the Fed helped organize the first-ever coordinated interest rate cut by the major central banks. The half-point reduction didn't reverse the erosion in market confidence, but it did signal an international commitment to easing monetary policy to promote growth, no small achievement considering the hawkish European Central Bank had just tightened policy in July. Hank and Ben, with support from Mervyn King of the Bank of England, also engineered a remarkably strong statement by the G-7 nations pledging "urgent and exceptional action" to end the crisis, forgoing the arcane jargon and diplomatic caveats that characterized most communiqués to commit that each country would "use all available tools to support systemically important financial institutions and prevent their failure." Our whatever-it-takes approach to the crisis was now the official policy of the major economies.

We still needed to finalize our capital program and the FDIC guarantees over Columbus Day weekend. Our challenge was to devise terms tough enough to protect taxpayers, but not so tough they would discourage participation by strong firms and stigmatize the program. We did not believe we could force firms with capital ratios above their regulatory minimums to participate in TARP, and we were worried that if only the weakest firms accepted government capital, the markets would run from those firms, while the rest of the system would remain undercapitalized and vulnerable. So while we did tighten some restrictions on CEO compensation that Congress had set as a condition for participation in TARP, we did not impose restrictions on compensation and bonuses for other bank executives. We wanted to maximize participation, so we could get enough capital into the system and broad enough guarantees to break the panic. We also made the terms of the capital injections compelling to the banks; Treasury would buy preferred stock with a 5 percent dividend increasing over time to 9 percent, with warrants (that is, options to buy additional stock at a fixed price in the future) that would ensure some upside for taxpayers if the firms did well. The goal was to make the capital attractive enough that all banks would accept it, but with incentives for them to replace it with private capital as market pressures eased.

For the guarantees, Bair agreed to apply the FDIC backstop to borrowing by bank holding companies as well as banks, charge fees low enough to avoid stigma, and guarantee debts in full rather than imposing haircuts—which, after all, would have defeated the purpose of the guarantees. But in order to reduce the FDIC's risk, she insisted that the backstop could apply only to new bank debt, which meant creditors would still have to worry about potential haircuts and defaults for existing debt—although the ability to issue new debt easily did make it more likely that the banks would be able to meet their obligations on the existing debt. Our capital plan was not all-powerful, either. By buying perpetual preferred stock, whose fixed dividend has to be paid before any dividends to common shareholders, we ran the risk that Treasury's capital injections would look more like loans than permanent equity investments, which could diminish market confidence that the system was being adequately recapitalized. Still, we were reasonably certain that TARP would attack liquidity as well as solvency problems, reducing the risk of runs while helping banks get healthy enough to start lending and promoting economic growth again. We believed it would also give the banks that needed more equity the breathing room to raise it from private investors without spooking the markets.

We needed to launch the program quickly with a show of overwhelming force, so on Columbus Day, Hank summoned the CEOs of nine of the most systemically important financial firms to the Treasury. The three of us, along with Bair and Comptroller of the Currency John Dugan, explained that we expected all nine of them to accept Treasury capital up to the equivalent of 3 percent of their risk-weighted assets, a total of $125 billion in TARP investments, along with FDIC guarantees of any new debt they issued through June 2009. It was a package deal: no government guarantees without the government capital. A few banks that considered themselves better capitalized were concerned that the program would make them look as weak as their more imperiled competitors, and all of the banks were reluctant to take on the government as an investor. But we reminded them that none of them should be confident they had enough capital to survive the severe recession that lay ahead, much less the runs that would accompany a meltdown of the system—and we would not give them the powerful guarantees unless they accepted our capital. All nine firms needed the system to survive, and the best way to ensure that was for all nine firms to participate in TARP. We would then make another $125 billion available to smaller banks, which wouldn't have to worry about stigma with the first nine on board. That afternoon, all nine CEOs accepted the TARP cash, and the stock market posted its biggest single-day point gain in history. In the ensuing months, we would move quickly to inject capital into nearly 700 smaller banks, a critically important step toward stabilizing and recapitalizing the entire banking system.

Ultimately, the government would earn a substantial return on its investments in U.S. banks, but at the time, the public thought we were giving away its money to the bankers who had just broken the economy. The Europeans took a more traditional approach to their banking problems that fall, nationalizing failing banks and offering capital to other banks at terms so punitive that few agreed to accept it. As a result, their banking system would remain woefully undercapitalized for years, and their economic recovery would be slower than ours. But the very attributes that would make TARP so successful in terms of its economic objectives would also increase its unpopularity with the American public, which understandably wanted us to punish the banks with the harshest possible terms.

And that was only the beginning of the end of the crisis.

We now had a more effective strategy in place to respond to the financial earthquake, but the economic tsunami was just reaching the shore. In the fourth quarter of 2008, the U.S. economy contracted at an 8.2 percent annual rate and shed nearly 2 million jobs, as the shocks on Wall Street began rippling through Main Street. Main Street's woes were in turn worsening the problems on Wall Street, as failing businesses defaulted on their loans and laid-off workers fell behind on their payments on credit cards, student loans, car loans, and mortgages. The troubled assets on bank balance sheets grew more troubled than ever, as increased mortgage defaults and delinquencies heightened concerns about mortgage-backed securities. The worst recession since the Depression was intensifying, further complicating our efforts to stabilize the financial system.

Critically, the TARP math was already turning ugly, prompting markets to wonder if our large new pot of money would be large enough to fill the system's remaining capital holes. We had only $350 billion in the initial tranche of TARP funding; we would need congressional approval to access the remaining $350 billion. So our injections of $250 billion into the banking sector left us just $100 billion in the first tranche of TARP and $450 billion overall. But a Fed analysis found the banking sector alone would need a further $290 billion in capital in a "stress scenario," and as much as $684 billion in an "extreme stress scenario." That didn't include the costs of helping home owners or rescuing the auto industry.

We also had to deal with AIG, which had posted shockingly large losses and was bleeding yet again. This time, we decided we needed to restructure its rescue package to try to cauterize its wounds in a more permanent way. Fortunately, we now had TARP, and Hank agreed to inject $40 billion in capital into the company to satisfy the credit rating agencies and the markets that it was financially viable. The Fed also provided financing for two new vehicles to take the risk of AIG's troubled securities off its balance sheets, roping off the assets that were shattering confidence in the firm. The Fed did test whether it could persuade AIG's major creditors to reduce the value of their claims on the company voluntarily, but they would not accept even extremely modest haircuts. In theory, we could have tried to compel them by threatening to force AIG into default, but our priority was to prevent a default and the downgrades and runs it would have triggered. Threatening default is not a great way to reduce fears of default, and we had no intention of fueling the panic by sending a message that no contract was safe.

It was a perilous time, made more dangerous by the fact that it was happening during the quadrennial holding period after the election of a new president. We had all been impressed by the responsible way Barack Obama handled the crisis during the campaign, and we knew he understood the magnitude of the challenge. He then signaled support for our whatever-it-takes strategy when he asked Tim to succeed Hank at Treasury, even though Tim had warned him the move would implicate him in our unpopular choices and complicate his message of change. Still, the ten-week transition between presidents felt unconscionably long. Hank and Ben took great comfort in Tim's nomination, but he had to recuse himself from dealing with financial institutions during the interregnum. And while Hank had talked to Obama regularly during the campaign, the president-elect did not continue those conversations during the transition. With guidance from Tim, Obama's other aides left Hank alone, too, invoking Washington's one-president-at-a-time rule, so decisions that would affect their administration were made without their input. At the time, Hank felt somewhat abandoned, but in retrospect, Obama did the right thing by letting the Bush administration and the Fed work without interference. And realistically, no incoming president would have wanted responsibility for some of the messy actions that had to be taken before his swearing-in.

The first emergency during the transition involved Citigroup, a global colossus with $2 trillion in assets. It was the weakest of the big banks, with a capital hole bigger than the injection it had received from TARP, and the markets knew it. It was way too large and interconnected to fail, so the Treasury agreed to use a further $20 billion in TARP capital to buy more preferred stock, this time with a stiffer 8 percent dividend. But more capital alone seemed unlikely to stop its creditors and uninsured foreign depositors from running. So the rescue also included a Fed and FDIC "ring fence" around $306 billion of Citi's worst assets, making the company responsible for the first $37 billion in potential losses, but providing a government guarantee for 90 percent of any losses above that. The idea was to limit Citi's tail risk by insuring it against a worst-case scenario, which would hopefully restore enough confidence to avert the worst-case scenario. We figured this approach would be much cheaper than injecting all the capital Citi needed or buying all its bad assets, unless the entire system collapsed—and in that case our problems would be much bigger than Citi.

At the same time, consumer credit markets were paralyzed, and the Fed and the Treasury had developed a program to revive them by jump-starting the markets for securities backed by consumer credit. So Ben and his Fed colleagues invoked 13(3) one more time to create the Term Asset-Backed Securities Loan Facility (TALF), which created demand for securities backed by credit card loans, student loans, car loans, and small business loans by accepting them as collateral for Fed loans to investors. The TALF program was backed by another $20 billion TARP investment in case the Fed suffered any losses on those securities, but it wouldn't end up absorbing any—and the program would help counteract the trend of banks restricting credit on Main Street when it was needed most.

After our commitments for bank capital, the AIG and Citi

rescues, and the consumer credit markets, we had almost exhausted our first $350 billion tranche of TARP. Meanwhile, Merrill Lynch was taking such extreme losses that Bank of America was threatening to back out of its merger, which seemed likely to trigger a run on both firms; even if the merger went through, we suspected we'd need TARP funds to save the combined company. TARP money would also be needed to rescue failing automakers in order to avert millions of potential layoffs in the industrial Midwest. TARP wasn't designed for industrial companies, which can usually declare bankruptcy and then restructure or liquidate in an orderly fashion, but the banking system was so fragile that the debtor-in-possession financing bankrupt firms rely on in normal times was unavailable. That meant a major bankruptcy could have triggered a meltdown of the entire industry and its supply chains. So in December, President Bush approved a total of $17.4 billion worth of bridge loans for General Motors and Chrysler, as well as deals to recapitalize and restructure their financing arms. This was basically a lifeline to keep the industry alive through the transition, although $4 billion was contingent on Congress's approving the second tranche of TARP.

The week before the end of his term, President Bush asked Congress to release that remaining $350 billion tranche, a politically unpleasant task he could have left to his Democratic successor. But Bush and Hank were determined to do all they could to defuse politically difficult problems (such as AIG, Citi, and Bank of America) so that Obama and his new team wouldn't have to, without making long-term decisions (such as deciding how the automakers should be restructured or how to help underwater home owners) that would have boxed in the new president. It would be hard to imagine a tougher time to navigate a financial and economic crisis than a presidential transition. At the time, the transition's logistical and political challenges seemed terribly frustrating. But in retrospect, it went surprisingly smoothly. Congress approved the second tranche of TARP without much drama.

And Hank and Ben engineered a rescue for Bank of America similar to Citi's, with $20 billion in capital from TARP and a ring fence around $118 billion of bad assets. These interventions stabilized the company. Fortunately, neither Bank of America nor Citi would ever have to make use of their special government guarantees, and both paid fees to the government for the protection they received.

The Bank of America rescue was Hank's last action as a public servant, although most of the crisis-fighting policies he had championed would continue after his departure. It was perhaps fitting that Hank and Ben were later accused of improperly pressuring Bank of America to close its Merrill Lynch deal, and had to testify under oath about the rescue of the bank. We would later have that privilege again during lawsuits filed by AIG's shareholders contending that the government should have preserved more of their equity when saving the company from collapse. The firms we rescued were not usually gracious about the terms of their rescues, while the overwhelming sentiment among the public was that they shouldn't have been rescued at all.

ENDGAME

Unfortunately, by the time President Obama took office the financial system was still unstable, and the economy was deteriorating badly. The TARP capital and guarantees were helping, and the banks would end up improving their earnings significantly in the first quarter, but there's always a lag before financial stabilization measures show up in economic data. The fear index that measures the risk of corporate defaults was even higher than it had been after the Lehman collapse. Consumer confidence was at an all-time low. When Tim met with the president for the first time as Treasury secretary, he warned Obama that Fannie Mae and Freddie Mac had almost burned through their $200 billion in federal aid and needed another $200 billion; that the markets still believed the financial system was seriously undercapitalized; and that AIG, Citi, and Bank of America were still wobbly despite their rescues. We had already distributed more than half of TARP, and doubt was spreading that we would be able to shore up the system and prevent more chaotic failures without another TARP. In fact, Obama's first budget proposal would include a $750 billion placeholder for additional financial rescues.

The Fed was doing its part to try to revive the economy. In December, it reduced its target short-term interest rate essentially to zero, where it would remain for the next seven years. Ben also announced plans for the Fed to buy $100 billion of debt issued by Fannie and Freddie along with $500 billion worth of mortgage-backed securities guaranteed by Fannie and Freddie. This was not only an effort to revive demand for the securities and boost the sagging housing market, but a signal that the Fed would continue to support growth in creative ways, even with the short-term interest rate constrained by its zero lower bound.

But more creativity from the Fed was not going to be enough. Even with interest rates at zero, even with TARP starting to weatherize banks for the building economic storm, the adverse feedback loop between economic decay and financial instability was in full swing. The new administration would pursue a variety of aggressive measures to jolt the economy back to life, including the largest fiscal stimulus bill in American history, an auto rescue plan that would force General Motors and Chrysler into receivership as a prelude to necessary restructuring, and more ambitious programs to reduce foreclosures and help home owners. At the same time, Obama wanted a forceful plan to fix the financial system so that it would no longer hold back the rest of the economy. In that initial Oval Office meeting, he told Tim he wasn't interested in waiting around and hoping things got better. He wanted action to get the financial problems out of the way now, so he could focus on addressing the other challenges created by the Great Recession.

The question was what kind of action. There was a growing belief among financial experts across the ideological spectrum that the banking sector was essentially unsalvageable, and that the president would be forced to nationalize some or all of it. Many of Tim's colleagues in the new administration shared that view, and persistent media leaks suggesting that nationalization looked inevitable had a debilitating effect on bank stocks. Investors were rushing to sell their shares before the government could dilute them or wipe them out.

Tim and Ben wanted to avoid a broad nationalization of the banking system unless it was absolutely necessary. And even nationalizing one or two major firms seemed likely to trigger panics that could lead to additional government takeovers. But with credit markets frozen and the recession getting worse, drift did not seem like a tenable strategy, either. After weeks of debate and consultation with his new team at Treasury, White House economic adviser Larry Summers and other Obama aides, the Fed, and the FDIC, Tim proposed a less drastic approach. His plan was designed to restore confidence in the health of banks with a mix of unprecedented transparency and new capital. Under this plan, the Fed and other bank regulators would identify, bank by bank, the size of the losses each institution might face in a severe recession and a renewed financial crisis. They would then disclose those loss estimates publicly and make sure each bank got enough capital to withstand those losses—from private sources if they could raise it, from TARP if they couldn't. Transparency was a risky strategy. If the experts were right, exposing the books of the banks to the sunlight would just unveil the depth of their insolvency to the world. But markets were already assuming the worst, acting as if the banks were the walking dead. Tim and his colleagues believed confidence would never return as long as uncertainty reigned, and they thought it was at least possible that perceptions of the health of the banking system were worse than reality.

The centerpiece of his plan would be the Supervisory Capital Assessment Program, or "the stress test." The Fed and other bank regulators would conduct rigorous reviews to determine whether major banks had enough capital to survive a depression-like downturn. Then it would make the results public, and banks that came up short would be given six months to raise the additional capital they needed. The ones that couldn't attract the investment privately would then be forced to accept additional TARP capital—and possibly government control. There was certainly a risk that many banks would end up in that situation, TARP would run out of money trying to recapitalize them, and large-scale nationalization would end up happening anyway. But preemptively putting the political system in charge of the banking system seemed like an extreme option when it was also possible that many banks were in better shape than the markets feared. Markets tend to overshoot on the way down as well as on the way up, and Tim was reluctant to turn banks into wards of the state based on fears of the unknown rather than proof they weren't viable. The stress test would provide a more accurate picture of the health of banks—and then would make sure the sick ones got the capital they needed, either voluntarily from investors or forcibly from TARP.

Tim and Ben also agreed on a dramatic expansion of TALF into a trillion-dollar Fed program backed by TARP funds, a move intended to broadcast the government's determination to resurrect the market for asset-backed securities. (As it turned out, this extra capacity would not be needed.) And Tim's team devised a new Treasury partnership with the private sector to buy troubled assets, adapting some of the ideas that Hank had put on hold in the rush to get TARP out the door. The Public-Private Investment Program (PPIP) would provide TARP loans to private investment firms that would decide which assets to buy and how much to pay, so the government wouldn't have to do it—but the investors would also have to put their own money at risk and share any profits with the government.

Tim unveiled his plan to break the back of the crisis in a speech on February 10. It was the first televised address of his career, and the markets plunged while he was still speaking. This was partly because Tim was vague about the details, which were still in flux, and partly because his delivery did not exactly inspire confidence; Barney Frank said he sounded like a boy at his bar mitzvah. Markets also may have been disappointed that Tim did not endorse ideas that were floating around for the government to buy troubled assets at inflated prices. In any case, there wasn't much Treasury or the Fed could do about the ugly reaction, except to design the new programs as fast as possible and hope the details would ultimately prove reassuring. The system would be in a frustrating limbo state until the programs were ready, and then again until the stress tests were done. We just had to hope it wouldn't collapse before the markets could see the results—or, for that matter, after.

In the meantime, the drumbeat for nationalization and haircuts continued, and we could feel the tremors in the markets with every fresh rumor and leak. In March, Obama convened a meeting of his economic team to debate the plan that Tim had already announced, because none of Tim's colleagues seemed happy with his approach. But none of them could articulate a workable alternative that would nationalize banks without sparking panic or draining TARP, and as Tim pointed out: Plan beats no plan. Obama ultimately agreed that it made more sense to supplement and adapt the stabilization programs that were already in place than to chart a radical new course, even though his political base wanted a bold break with the Bush years. The potential downsides of the stress test were obvious; there was no guarantee that the answers it produced would be conducive to calm. But there was a reasonable chance that forcing the entire system to prepare for a depression-like event would reduce the likelihood of that depression-like event, and that its triage would help draw a bright line between fundamentally healthy banks and terminally ill banks.

It would all depend on the stress test results. Some skeptics expected the test to be a sham, in which the Fed would subject the banks to a gentle scenario engineered to get them a clean bill of health. But we knew that if the stress test didn't seem credible, the markets would keep assuming the worst regardless of the results. The scenario the Fed would actually use was quite brutal, envisioning loan losses even worse than the losses during the Great Depression, and housing price decreases that turned out to be even worse than the reality of 2009. Tim's Treasury colleagues also came up with a critical tweak to limit the uncertainty of the waiting period, fixing the price that Treasury would pay for stock in undercapitalized banks at February levels, even if the price fell further before the stress tests were complete. That condition, which Tim's staff dubbed the "Geithner put," reduced the incentive for investors to run away from banks while the Fed was still poring through their books.

The waiting period was still excruciating. Citi faltered again, and Treasury had to engineer a complex deal with some of its private stockholders to bolster its capital buffer without nationalizing the bank. Then AIG needed yet another TARP lifeline, this time for $30 billion—just before it revealed it was paying lavish taxpayer-funded bonuses to some of its employees, triggering the most ferocious public backlash of the entire crisis. The rollout of Treasury's PPIP program to buy troubled assets was also attacked as a scandalous boondoggle for private investors, although it would also end up generating a modest positive return for taxpayers. Meanwhile, although the economy was still in terrible shape, with unemployment rising to 8.9 percent by the end of April, the pace of the deterioration was slowing.

In May, the Fed released the results of its stress test, and they were much better than many in the markets had expected. The Fed determined that nine of the nineteen largest financial firms were already adequately capitalized to withstand the test's worst-case scenario, and the other ten needed, collectively, only about $75 billion in additional capital. The Fed released the underlying data that demonstrated how it had reached its conclusions, and the market considered the results credible. The cost of insuring against defaults by financial institutions quickly dropped, and the private sector once again regained the confidence it needed to invest in banks. Within a month, the undercapitalized firms had raised almost all the capital they needed to comply with the stress test mandate. The only firm that couldn't was GMAC, so Treasury would fill the gap with a relatively modest infusion of TARP funds. Ultimately, even the rescue of GMAC—now known as Ally Bank—would generate a $2.4 billion profit for the Treasury. As late as April 2009, the International Monetary Fund was still predicting that the U.S. government would spend $2 trillion rescuing its banking system. But TARP's capital programs for banks and insurers would end up earning about $50 billion for the Treasury, and overall, our financial interventions would produce a substantially larger direct financial return, on top of the huge economic benefits from having a functioning, rather than a collapsing, financial system.

The stress test was a somewhat anticlimactic conclusion to a twenty-month ordeal, finally reassuring the markets there would be no more Lehmans. It was not a magic solution that ended the crisis; it was the culmination of a long series of emergency interventions that made the end of the crisis possible. The Fed's far-flung lending and liquidity programs, the rescues of Bear, Fannie, Freddie, and AIG, the Treasury's guarantee of money market funds, the FDIC's guarantees of bank debt, and the initial deployment of TARP funds to banks were all necessary to put out the fire, even though none of those actions was sufficient on its own. If not for all those interventions—especially the hundreds of billions of dollars' worth of capital that TARP had already pumped into the banking system, along with the private capital we had pressured banks to raise since the crisis began—the results of the stress test would have been much less reassuring to the markets and much more expensive for taxpayers.

What's more, if all these aggressive actions to fix the financial system hadn't been supplemented by similarly aggressive actions to revive the broader economy, the gains achieved by the dramatic innovations in strategy on and around Columbus Day would have been squandered and eroded. Eventually, the full force of the U.S. government proved to be enough to put out the fire, but just barely. Anything less would not have been enough.

Just as an irreversible financial collapse would have plunged the economy into depression, a prolonged economic free fall would have forced the financial system into collapse. Our financial interventions worked only in tandem with an aggressive effort to resuscitate economic demand in early 2009—more monetary boldness from the Fed, unprecedented fiscal stimulus from Obama and Congress, a government rescue of the auto industry, and a flawed but still substantial push to revive the housing market and help vulnerable home owners. We eventually restored normalcy by using all the financial and economic weapons at our disposal, and they were all the more powerful because they were deployed together.

In a provocative speech back in 2002, Ben had argued that even at the zero lower bound, when central banks traditionally had run out of economic ammunition, they could use unorthodox measures to fight deflationary and recessionary pressures. But in 2009, the economy badly needed more help, and in early March, the Fed launched an aggressive monetary stimulus experiment known as "quantitative easing," buying mortgage securities and then Treasury bonds to try to bring down long-term interest rates and fight the Great Recession. The initial round, "QE1," would expand to $1.75 trillion in Fed purchases and send a confidence-inducing message that the Fed would not stand by and let the economy stagnate. Ben and his colleagues would announce QE2 and QE3 in 2010 and 2012, eventually expanding the Fed's balance sheet to more than $4.5 trillion, nearly five times its pre-crisis peak. A wide range of academic studies have found that quantitative easing lowered long-term Treasury and mortgage rates and helped support the economic recovery; it also encouraged other central banks to adopt similar programs to support global growth.

Alongside the effects of the Fed's monetary policy actions, the new administration poured fiscal stimulus into the Main Street economy through the American Recovery and Reinvestment Act of 2009, an enormous package of $300 billion in temporary tax cuts along with $500 billion worth of new federal spending—including relief to victims of the recession; public works designed to provide jobs while upgrading the nation's infrastructure; and direct aid to states to prevent them from raising taxes, cutting budgets, and deepening the Great Recession. Congressional Republicans almost unanimously opposed the package, attacking Obama as an out-of-control spender, but most independent economists agree that the Recovery Act helped save jobs, boost growth, and end the recession by June 2009. State and local governments—most of which faced balanced-budget requirements—did offset some of its power with tax hikes, layoffs, and spending cuts, but it helped launch growth in the United States while other developed economies were still shrinking. Normally, governments should try to live within their means, but when private demand collapses, aggressive deficit spending that can jolt the economy to life is more fiscally responsible than government belt-tightening that further reduces demand. Brutal recessions can blow up deficits for years; stimulus packages that boost deficits in the short term but help workers earn taxable income again and businesses make taxable profits again can reduce deficits in the long run.

The country could have afforded and the economy could have used an even larger stimulus package, but there were only 60 votes in the Senate for $800 billion, and there was no filibuster-proof support for anything larger. Congressional Democrats did quietly follow up with a dozen more modest stimulus measures cutting payroll taxes, expanding unemployment aid, and sending more help to states, ultimately injecting a further $657 billion into the economy. The Obama administration also poured more TARP money into an aggressive and controversial auto rescue plan that forced General Motors and Chrysler into receivership as a prelude to long-overdue restructuring. Overall, the auto industry would receive more than $80 billion from TARP, but in the end, the cost to taxpayers would be only $9.3 billion, a relatively small price to pay to salvage a vital U.S. manufacturing sector. Between 2008 and 2012, the federal fiscal expansion (including automatic countercyclical stabilizers as well as discretionary stimulus) amounted to about 3.4 percent of GDP per year. The tax cuts and government transfers were also progressive in their impact, almost fully offsetting the aggregate decline in income experienced by families in the bottom 40 percent of the income distribution.

Tim and his colleagues in the Obama administration also launched a series of new programs to support the housing market, building on the programs to recapitalize Fannie and Freddie and the Fed's actions to lower mortgage interest rates. The day after the Recovery Act became law, the president unveiled a housing strategy that included the Home Affordable Refinance Program (HARP), to help "underwater" home owners refinance their mortgages even though they owed more than their homes were currently worth, and the Home Affordable Modification Program (HAMP), to help delinquent home owners modify their monthly payments. Hank and the Bush administration had initiated several private-sector mortgage modification efforts, but their scope had been limited by their voluntary nature and the unavailability of federal funding. Obama's efforts backed by TARP dollars were seen as a clear escalation—so much so that they inspired the CNBC personality Rick Santelli's famous on-air rant calling for a new anti-government Tea Party to protest bailouts for freeloading home owners. The progressive left felt just as strongly that the government's response to the foreclosure crisis was weak and late, a betrayal of Main Street.

These programs were painfully slow and disappointing in their reach. HARP, after a glacial start, would eventually help more than 3 million home owners refinance their mortgages, while nearly 25 million more would take advantage of low rates to refinance without government assistance. HAMP was a logistical nightmare, reliant on a dysfunctional loan servicing industry that routinely lost paperwork, failed to return phone calls, and generally gave borrowers the runaround. Tim's team at Treasury thought about setting up its own servicing program from scratch but decided there wasn't enough time, and banks were reluctant to invest in the infrastructure they would have needed to identify the mortgages that were suited for modifications and get the deals done quickly. HAMP also had onerous compliance requirements and restrictive eligibility rules to protect against fraud, which further bogged down an already unwieldy process and persuaded banks to restructure millions of mortgages privately without the HAMP subsidy rather than deal with the government red tape. Ultimately, HAMP would directly support only a fraction of Obama's goal of 3 million to 4 million mortgage modifications, but in the end the combination of government and private-sector modifications reached more than 8 million home owners.

The struggles of HARP and HAMP got a lot of attention and convinced many observers that the government's housing policies had failed. The federal actions that had the greatest impact on housing were the $400 billion lifeline for Fannie Mae and Freddie Mac, which kept mortgage credit flowing after private capital abandoned the field, and the Fed's aggressive purchases of mortgage-backed securities, which helped keep mortgage rates low and facilitated refinancings. Programs to reduce foreclosures after a real estate crash and a deep recession were much tougher to design. The politics were treacherous, and there was no easy way to craft targeted programs to help financially distressed home owners stay in their homes without wasting money on home owners who either didn't need help or would never be able to afford their homes even with government help.

The preferred option of many housing activists was a "principal reduction" program that would reduce the amount that underwater home owners owed. But the government couldn't just force banks to forgive mortgage debt, and providing sufficient incentives for them to do so voluntarily would have been an incredibly inefficient use of tax dollars. One 2014 study in the *Brookings Papers on Economic Activity* found that if the government had spent an additional $700 billion to wipe out every dollar of negative equity in the U.S. real estate market, it would have had very little impact on the broader economy, increasing personal consumption by less than 0.2 percent and costing an estimated $1.5 million for each job it saved. By contrast, TARP's support for the auto industry would cost about $14,000 per job saved. The Obama administration did push the Federal Housing Finance Agency to pursue some targeted principal reduction for Fannie and Freddie loans, but the independent agency resisted. What proved the more effective approach, rather than reducing mortgage principal, was to reduce monthly payments, the approach taken by most private- as well as public-sector loan modifications.

Ultimately, the government response to the housing slump was effective in the broader sense of stabilizing the housing and mortgage markets overall. Without the nationalization of Fannie and Freddie or the Fed and Treasury purchases of mortgage securities, house prices would have fallen dramatically further, millions more Americans would have lost their homes, and the recession would have been much worse. The programs designed to help individual home owners refinance their homes or modify their mortgages also reached millions, but they were slow to get moving and limited in scope. Congress was never enthusiastic about a dramatically more powerful housing strategy, and Tim and most of those in the Obama administration also believed that additional dollars spent on unemployment benefits, infrastructure projects, payroll tax cuts, and aid to states would have more economic bang for the buck—while raising fewer dilemmas about fairness—than a new wave of programs aimed narrowly at home owners. Solving the economic crisis was a necessary condition for solving the housing crisis, while the reverse was not necessarily true. In the end, a long and steady economic recovery might be the most successful housing program. Home prices stabilized after the Great Recession ended, gradually eliminating trillions of dollars of negative equity, lifting millions of underwater home owners above water.

The better economy made almost everything better. U.S. annual auto sales had plunged to 10 million in 2009, but they were back up to pre-crisis levels of 17 million by 2015. The credit crunch ended for most consumers and businesses, although banks remained skittish about lending for longer than we would have liked, especially to potential home buyers. Unemployment came down rapidly from a peak of 10.0 percent in late 2009 to 3.7 percent as we write, and the economy that was shedding more than 2 million jobs a quarter in early 2009 has added some 19 million jobs over a record ninety-seven consecutive months. Corporate profits recovered rapidly, much faster than wages did, but child poverty rates declined to historic lows. Compared with other countries in this crisis or historical recoveries from past crises, the recession was much less severe and the recovery began much earlier in the United States. And although the recovery wasn't as strong as many had hoped, it has been unusually steady.

Still, the crisis of 2008 inflicted tremendous pain. It is often incorrectly blamed for rising inequality, wage stagnation, and other economic trends that had festered for decades before getting masked by the boom, but it is correctly blamed for millions of layoffs, millions of foreclosures, and lingering trauma for millions of families. We wish we had been able to put out the fire quicker than we did, but we are grateful that the United States was able to prevent an economic catastrophe that could have rivaled the Great Depression.

And we remain worried about the risk of the next fire.

CONCLUSION

THE FIRE NEXT TIME

NONE OF US, NOR ANY OF OUR ACCOMPLISHED COLLEAGUES, had ever lived through a crisis like this one. And despite Ben's expertise on the Great Depression, Hank's feel for financial markets, and Tim's experience with crises abroad, none of us was ever sure what would work, what would backfire, or how much stress the system would be able to handle. There was no standard playbook we could consult for guidance, no professional consensus about best practices. We had to feel our way through the fog, sometimes changing our tactics, sometimes changing our minds, with enormous uncertainty about the outcomes. And many of the things we did appeared to reward the very financial industry that had dragged the world into the crisis in the first place.

So it was understandable and perhaps inevitable that commentators tended to assume, and predict, the worst. Critics warned that we were setting the stage for a run on the dollar, or Zimbabwe-style hyperinflation, or a Greece-style debt crisis, or trillions of dollars in bailout costs, or a Japan-style system dominated by unsalvageable zombie banks, or even the death of American free-market capitalism. Ultimately, none of that happened—not in spite of our choices, we believe, but because of them. We were fortunate that Congress eventually gave us expanded powers that allowed us to mobilize a forceful and effective response—and perhaps, in some ways, we were simply fortunate. But with a decade to reflect on what happened here as well as in other countries in this crisis, we believe that the strategy the United States adopted, and we helped shape, worked about as well as could have been hoped, given the constraints and radical uncertainties the country faced. The stress of the 2008 crisis was in some ways—including the declines in stock prices and home prices, and the falls in output and employment—even worse than the early stages of the Great Depression, but this time the government managed to stop the panic, stabilize the financial system, revive the credit markets, and jump-start a recovery that continues to this day. The U.S. recovery compares favorably to recoveries from previous severe financial crises and the recoveries of other advanced economies from this crisis.

Although it could well have been worse, the crisis was still extraordinarily damaging, for both the United States and the world. Millions of Americans lost their jobs, their businesses, their savings, and their homes. One crucial lesson of 2008 is that financial crises can be devastating even when the response is relatively aggressive and benefits from the formidable financial strength and credibility of the United States. The best strategy for a financial crisis is not to have one. And the best way to limit the damage if there is one is to make sure crisis managers have the tools they need to fight before things get too bad.

Unfortunately, financial crises will never be entirely preventable, because they are products of human emotions and perceptions, as well as the inevitable lapses of human regulators and policymakers. Finance depends on confidence, and confidence is always fragile. While it's vital to try to rein in excessive leverage and risk taking on Wall Street, that leverage and risk taking is generally a reflection of excess optimism in society as a whole. Regulators and policymakers aren't immune to those manias. Human beings are inherently susceptible to irrational exuberance as well as irrational fears, and markets that overshoot on the way up tend to overshoot on the way down. Mania and panic both seem to be contagious.

But that's not an argument for passivity or inaction before a crisis hits. Even though there's no silver bullet capable of eradicating financial crises forever, there's a lot government officials can do to try to reduce the vulnerability of the financial system to crises, and to make crises less frequent and less likely to spiral out of control. The U.S. government was not well prepared for the fire of 2008, which helps explain why it burned so hot, why the efforts to contain it often seemed so messy, and even why that response became so wildly unpopular. Better preparation could have created better outcomes. If the regulatory system had been less balkanized and more capable of addressing the risks outside commercial banks, if crisis managers had been empowered all along to use overwhelming force to avoid financial collapse, and if there had been mechanisms in place from the start to ensure that the financial system would pay for its own rescue, the fire would have been less intense, and the firefighting would have seemed less inconsistent and unfair.

A decade later, the vital question to ask is whether the United States is better prepared today. We believe the answer is: yes and no. There are better safeguards in place to avoid a panic in the first place—the financial equivalent of more aggressive fire prevention measures and stronger fire-resistant building codes. But the emergency authorities for government officials to respond when an intense crisis does happen are in many ways even weaker than they were in 2007—the financial equivalent of less-well-equipped firefighters and shuttered firehouses. The government's ability to respond to a collapse in economic demand with monetary and fiscal stimulus—its so-called Keynesian arsenal—has also been significantly depleted. In short, the U.S. economy and financial system today may be less prone to modest brush fires but more vulnerable to a major inferno if, despite updated and improved fire codes, a conflagration were to begin. To use a different analogy, it's as if policymakers had reacted to a public health disaster by expanding immunizations, promoting good nutrition, and encouraging annual checkups—but also decided to shut down emergency rooms and outlaw life-saving surgeries.

STRONGER DEFENSES

It's worth recapping why the system was so unsafe before the 2008 crisis, because it helps illuminate the path toward greater safety now. Again, the basic problems were too much risky leverage, too much runnable short-term financing, and the migration of too much risk to shadow banks where regulation was negligible and the Fed's emergency safety net was inaccessible. There were also too many major firms that were too big and interconnected to fail without threatening the stability of the system, and the explosion of opaque mortgage-backed derivatives had turned the health of the housing market into a potential vector for panic. Meanwhile, America's regulatory bureaucracy was fragmented and outdated, with no one responsible for monitoring and addressing systemic risks.

Nobody knows exactly what the next financial crisis will look like, but historically, crises have followed a similar mania-panic-crash pattern of excessive risk taking and leverage. After the crisis, Ben and Tim thought the most important safeguards would be stricter limits on the risk firms could take with borrowed money. That meant requiring them to hold more loss-absorbing capital—Tim's mantra was "capital, capital, capital"—and take on less leverage, the flip side of capital. That also meant more conservative liquidity requirements, forcing lenders to hold more cash and other liquid assets while relying less on short-term financing that could run at the first sign of trouble. The largest firms, which would pose the greatest danger if they defaulted on their obligations, would be subject to even tougher constraints on their risk taking and their funding. Most important, the new rules would have to be applied more broadly across the financial system, not only in the United States but around the world, with flexibility to expand them further in the future to help prevent the migration of risk outside the perimeter of the rules toward the path of least regulatory resistance.

The Obama administration and the Fed worked hard to achieve those goals, negotiating with Congress over the Dodd-Frank Wall Street Reform and Consumer Protection Act of 2010 for the United States, while leading a global effort to apply tougher constraints on risk taking across the largest economies. And in those areas, the negotiations produced much more robust defenses against potential crises. The Basel III global regulatory regime tripled the minimum capital requirements for banks and quadrupled them for the largest banks, while also requiring higher-quality capital that could truly absorb losses, ensuring that the global system would have much hardier shock absorbers. The standards the Fed crafted for U.S. banks were even tougher. Liquidity requirements were also enhanced worldwide, reducing the reliance of financial institutions on unstable overnight funding. Before the crisis, uninsured short-term liabilities amounted to about one third of the assets in the financial system; today they are only about one sixth. The repo market is much smaller, the assets it finances are much safer, and intraday credit, the riskiest element of repo, is down 90 percent from the pre-crisis peak.

Not only are these risk-taking restrictions tougher, they are also broader, applying not only to traditional commercial banks but to broker-dealers and other nonbanks that used to operate in the shadows. Before the crisis, firms holding only 42 percent of the assets in the financial system faced significant constraints on their leverage; now that figure has risen to 88 percent. Furthermore, the reforms targeted financial instruments and funding markets as well as individual firms. For example, Dodd-Frank required most derivatives to be traded openly on public exchanges rather than negotiated in private deals, reducing the danger that uncertainty about which firms are exposed to which risks would again stoke panic. The law also imposed more conservative margin requirements for derivatives trades, repo borrowing, and securities lending, another way of discouraging excessive speculation. The average daily volume of securities lending dropped from $2.5 trillion to $1 trillion between 2008 and 2015. And several risky classes of funding vehicles that created problems for institutions like Bear Stearns and Citi got wiped out during the crisis and have not reemerged.

The post-crisis reforms also tried to limit the risk that the failure of a large bank could destabilize the broader system. A "systemic surcharge" on the largest banks requires them to hold more capital than smaller institutions against a given amount of risk, reducing their ability to take on leverage and increasing their buffers against losses. Dodd-Frank also included language barring mergers that would concentrate more than 10 percent of the system's liabilities in a single bank, empowering the Fed to break up banks it considered a serious threat to the stability of the system, and requiring the Fed to conduct annual stress tests of big banks to make sure they're prepared for the most adverse economic and financial scenarios. In 2018, some bipartisan tweaks from Congress raised the threshold for firms to face automatic stress tests from $50 billion to $250 billion in assets, but the Fed still has the power to test any firm it considers a potential systemic threat. As time passes and memories fade, it will be vital that the inevitable pressures to push the pendulum back toward a softer approach do not recreate the vulnerabilities that existed before the crisis. But so far, virtually all of the core Dodd-Frank reforms remain in place, and while some critics initially attacked them as a massive overreach that would cripple the financial system, the system has proved strong enough to support a sustained economic expansion.

Other critics attacked the Dodd-Frank reforms for preserving too much of the status quo instead of breaking up big banks immediately and reinstating the Depression-era Glass-Steagall Act rules that separated commercial banking from more speculative investment banking. Those more radical measures would have been heavy lifts in Congress, but that's not why we didn't pursue them. We simply didn't believe they would address the root causes of the crisis or limit the risk of future crises. After all, Bear Stearns, Lehman Brothers, Fannie Mae, Freddie Mac, and AIG were nonbanks that would have been unaffected by Glass-Steagall, while Wachovia and Washington Mutual were banks that got into trouble the old-fashioned way, by making bad loans. Bigness is not always a negative; the crisis would have been much worse if JPMorgan, Bank of America, and Wells Fargo hadn't been huge enough to swallow not-quite-as-huge Bear, WaMu, Countrywide, Merrill Lynch, and Wachovia before they collapsed. And smallness is not always a positive; a cascade of failures by relatively tiny banks helped trigger the Great Depression. In any case, the nation's largest banks have performed quite well over their first eight years of stress testing under Dodd-Frank. In 2018, the Fed concluded they would still have more capital *after* a severe global recession with losses larger than those experienced in the 2007–2009 crisis than they had during the good times *before* the crisis. And a report back in 2014 by the Government Accountability Office, commissioned by congressional critics who expected it to prove the too-big-to-fail problem was worse than ever, found the biggest banks could no longer borrow at much lower rates than small banks, a sign markets are less convinced that they are too big to fail.

We would have liked to see more restructuring of the antiquated financial regulatory system, a key element of Hank's original blueprint for reform, with the Fed in charge of monitoring systemic risks and several redundant agencies consolidated to create more consistency and accountability. But the political turf battles were daunting, and this felt like a war of choice rather than a war of necessity. The Fed faced a fierce backlash after the crisis, and Congress had no interest in giving it sweeping new powers. Dodd-Frank did create a Financial Stability Oversight Council (FSOC) of regulators led by the Treasury secretary, which at least made one government body, though not a single agency, responsible for assessing and limiting risks across the financial system. And the FSOC does have the power to act to minimize systemic risks it detects, including the power to designate any financial institution as "systemically important" and therefore subject to stricter supervision by the Fed. Dodd-Frank also took a tentative step toward reorganization by abolishing the Office of Thrift Supervision, the perennially captured regulator of Countrywide, WaMu, and AIG. Otherwise, though, every agency in the federal org chart survived. Tim initially hoped to merge the SEC, the watchdog for securities markets, with the CFTC, the overseer of derivatives markets, but turf wars between the congressional committees overseeing the two agencies made the idea a political nonstarter.

Dodd-Frank even added an agency to that cluttered org chart: the Consumer Financial Protection Bureau, which consolidated the consumer protection divisions of all the other regulators into one powerful new cop on the financial beat. But it made sense to create a one-stop shop for consumer protection, which had often languished inside agencies with other priorities. Aggressive enforcement of fraud in consumer credit markets, in addition to helping ordinary Americans keep more of their money, could enhance financial stability as well, by cracking down on the kind of shoddy underwriting and other predatory behaviors that caused so many problems in the mortgage market.

Together, these reforms should reduce the frequency of crises. The new rules are already forcing financial institutions, especially larger financial institutions, to hold more and higher-quality capital, accumulate less leverage, and finance themselves in safer ways—and annual stress tests are making sure they're preparing for worst-case scenarios. The derivatives market is less evocative of the Wild West, consumer protections have been enhanced, and there is finally a government body responsible for monitoring potential dangers to the entire system.

But stronger rules and stricter oversight will never prevent all financial crises. Vigilant regulators can recognize warning signs, especially extended credit booms, but they can never be sure which booms reflect manias or when those manias will flip into panics. Even if the new rules somehow keep up with innovations in financial markets, they won't eradicate human frailty or herd behavior, so they won't stop every long wave of optimism and complacency from overcorrecting into a crisis of confidence. Policymakers need to have humility about their ability to identify and correct dangerously contagious beliefs, or to prevent them from sparking panics. If bubbles were as easy to identify as many seem to think, investors would never get caught up in them.

Even thick capital buffers, the most robust defense against unexpected adversity, can be inadequate protections against all-out runs. As we saw in 2008, capital cushions can seem safe and adequate until suddenly they aren't. The amount of private capital U.S. banks have raised since the crisis would have been enough to cover all their losses during the crisis, a welcome step toward safety, but those losses would have been much worse if Washington's forceful use of monetary and fiscal stimulus hadn't staunched the economic bleeding. And as the traumas of 2008 recede further into the distance, extended periods of stability could encourage renewed complacency, policymakers may be tempted to soften the post-crisis restrictions on risk taking, and markets could again get comfortable financing significant amounts of maturity transformation outside the perimeter of strict regulatory oversight. It's worth remembering how much leveraged risk taking migrated away from banks before the crisis, even when capital requirements were much lower. Now the incentives to find new opportunities for regulatory arbitrage are even stronger, and regulation tends to fall behind the curve.

It's certainly conceivable that the world will get better at anticipating and preempting shocks. Central banks and international institutions have invested heavily in financial stability units that try to identify danger signs through "big data" illustrated with elaborate "heat maps," and we wish them well. But we suspect that neither high-tech monitoring nor prudential supervision will fully protect the financial system from the failures of imagination and limitations of memory that seem hardwired in human beings. Eventually, a threat will be overlooked and a crisis will erupt. As the New York Fed's Meg McConnell likes to say, we spend a lot of time looking for systemic risk, but it tends to find us. That's when government responders need a safety net, and we're afraid America's is even more riddled with holes than it was before the crisis.

WEAKER EMERGENCY ARSENAL

The story of how the crisis happened is a complex story about risky leverage, runnable funding, shadow banking, rampant securitization, and outdated regulation. But the story of how the crisis got so terrible is a comparatively simple story about the weak and antiquated arsenal of emergency weapons we had to fight it.

When Tim started at the New York Fed in 2003, he read its "Doomsday Book" outlining its break-the-glass emergency powers, and he wasn't impressed. Ben had a similar experience when he became Fed chairman in 2006 and asked for a briefing on crisis-fighting tools. The Fed had broad powers to lend to banks against solid collateral, but it could only lend to nonbanks in a crisis if it invoked its 13(3) emergency powers, and even then only if the potential borrowers were near or past the point of no return. Its authority was surprisingly crimped; for example, its power to buy financial assets was limited to Treasuries and low-risk securities guaranteed by Fannie Mae and Freddie Mac, while other central banks could buy much riskier securities and in some cases equities. And as Hank learned, Treasury had virtually no standing authority to intervene in a crisis, which was a problem, because systemic crises don't just peter out. There's no way to quell a severe panic without government action that substitutes sovereign credit for private credit and assumes losses the market won't bear. No private institution can self-insure against a one-hundred-year flood.

During the crisis, the Fed stretched its lender-of-last-resort programs to the edges of its authority, and they proved to be effective tools for providing liquidity to cash-strapped institutions and propping up faltering credit markets. But conventional and even unconventional lending cannot magically restore confidence in troubled firms or troubled assets during a truly systemic crisis. The Fed also reinterpreted its emergency lending authority in creative ways to avert catastrophic collapses of Bear Stearns and AIG, but those last-ditch rescues didn't restore confidence in the financial system, either, because the government had no way to reassure investors and creditors that other major firms wouldn't face similar collapses. Walter Bagehot had made the powerful case for why central banks should lend to viable firms against good collateral. This crisis illustrated the limits of Bagehot's doctrine. We had to go to Congress at the height of the crisis to get the authority we needed to recapitalize endangered firms, and even then it took time and transparency to reassure the markets that there was no longer a reason to run. We believe that if we had started the crisis with that authority, even if carefully hedged and constrained, we could have acted more forcefully, more swiftly, and more comprehensively, with interventions designed to help restore confidence in the entire system. Instead, we had to rely for most of the crisis on the more limited Fed liquidity tools and ad hoc rescues that kept us from getting out in front of the crisis.

After the crisis, Tim and Ben hoped to preserve the new powers we had used to stabilize the system and secure additional authority for first responders to wind down systemically dangerous institutions in an orderly fashion in future crises. The Obama administration also proposed even stronger guarantee powers for the FDIC, to reduce the likelihood of a Lehman-type failure and reduce the need for the Fed to orchestrate one-off rescues of individual firms like Bear and AIG. But the TARP authority expired, and the final congressional version of Dodd-Frank curtailed rather than expanded the government's firefighting tools. The FDIC's broad guarantee authority, so effective during the crisis, was eliminated, as was the ability of the Fed to lend to individual nonbank financial firms under its 13(3) emergency powers. The Fed retained the ability under 13(3) to lend to broad classes of institutions, as it had done for primary dealers, and to support important funding markets, as it had done for commercial paper, but with less discretion and less ability to take risk than before. For example, Congress limited the Fed's discretion to judge when its loans are secured to its satisfaction, making it harder for the central bank to accept risky collateral in a future emergency. There was simply no political support for anything that could have been construed as enabling future bailouts.

In general, the crisis managers of tomorrow will have less authority and less flexibility to take action to support the financial system than we had. Congress took away the Treasury's power to use the Exchange Stabilization Fund to issue guarantees, even though that power protected the savings of ordinary Americans and vital short-term funding for much of corporate America when money market funds were melting down after the Reserve Primary Fund broke the buck. Congress also curtailed the executive branch's ability to take credit risk alongside the Fed, as it had done to backstop consumer credit markets through the Term

Asset-Backed Securities Loan Facility. Dodd-Frank even weakened the Fed's traditional lender-of-last-resort programs, adding disclosure rules that, whatever their benefits in terms of transparency, will increase the potential stigma of taking loans from the Fed, making it harder for the Fed to inject liquidity into the system in future crises.

Dodd-Frank did create one important new piece of firefighting equipment, "orderly liquidation authority," a bankruptcy-like mechanism for failing complex firms that would allow crisis managers to wind them down without triggering a chaotic collapse, as the FDIC already does for smaller and simpler banks. Our inability to do this during the crisis was a frequent source of frustration—and during Lehman weekend, a source of disaster. The Fed had to stretch its lending authority to avoid a messy failure of Bear, an intervention that worked only because JPMorgan was capable of standing behind Bear's obligations, and we had no recourse when we couldn't find a similar buyer for Lehman. The goal of crisis management should not be to prevent all failures, but rather to prevent uncontrolled failures of systemic firms in the midst of a general panic. A well-crafted resolution authority could be an elegant way to avoid chaos while helping to ensure that no financial institution is too big to fail.

We won't know how well this new resolution authority will work until it's used, and the three of us do not entirely agree on its promise. We certainly don't want to dismiss the importance of the new resolution regime, or the associated "living wills" that systemically important firms must draw up in good times to help the government wind them down in case of disaster. But it's fair to say that the new authority is likely to be more effective in managing the failure of a Lehman-type firm in an otherwise stable environment than when other firms are also in danger and the entire system is on the edge of panic.

Overall, while the United States has much stronger safeguards against the occurrence of panic than it had before the crisis, it has weaker emergency authorities for responding when a panic occurs. Its crisis managers lack the power to inject capital, guarantee liabilities, or purchase assets without going to Congress. Meanwhile, the Fed has lost its power to rescue individual firms and faces new constraints on its lending powers, while the Treasury has lost its ability to use the Exchange Stabilization Fund for guarantees. This has all been done in the name of avoiding government rescues, a worthy goal. But the better way to avoid government rescues is not to hobble the first responders but to avoid crises in the first place. Eventually, risk tends to weave its way around even the best-designed safeguards, but that is a reason to give crisis managers the authority they need to respond with overwhelming force. You can't wish away fires by closing the firehouse.

Of course, when an epic crisis does arrive, Congress would have the power to undo the preemptive limitations it has placed on crisis managers. But that is easier said than done in a nonparliamentary democracy where legislative changes require support from the president, the House of Representatives, and a filibuster-proof majority in the Senate. At a minimum, financial firefighters would have to follow our tortuous path of spending time, energy, and political capital to get the trucks and hoses they need while the fire is already burning, which can intensify crises and increase their ultimate costs to taxpayers and the economy. And it's hard to look at the bitterly polarized politics of modern America and feel confident that a bipartisan consensus for unpopular but necessary actions would emerge when it mattered most.

As bad as the crisis and subsequent recession were, they would have been much worse if the Federal Reserve, the Congress, and the executive branch had not engineered massive monetary and fiscal stimulus to stop the contraction and aid the recovery. Another key lesson of 2008 was that even aggressive measures to stabilize the financial system can't succeed if the economy is imploding, while aggressive measures to revive the economy can't succeed if the financial system is collapsing. Crisis fighting and macroeconomic policies have to work together, and a government's ability to limit the intensity of a financial crisis depends on its macroeconomic room for maneuver.

Fortunately, before the crisis, America's Keynesian arsenal was reasonably well stocked. The Fed had plenty of room to lower interest rates and pursue other expansionary monetary policies, while the rest of the government had the budgetary space to undertake expansionary fiscal policies like tax cuts and increased spending. Today, the Keynesian arsenal looks far more constrained, which could be a significant handicap in a serious crisis. And while the Fed has gradually raised interest rates, which will help replenish the monetary ammunition it deployed during the last crisis, Washington's political branches are squandering their fiscal ammunition when they ought to be gathering more.

On the monetary side, the United States entered the crisis with the federal funds rate at 5.25 percent, modest by historical standards but comfortably above zero—and Ben had already suggested he'd be willing to take unorthodox actions to support a flagging economy when the federal funds rate hit the zero lower bound. The Fed may have been a bit too tentative in the early months of the crisis, but it cut rates more quickly than any other central bank starting in early 2008. It lowered rates to the zero lower bound during the darkest days of the fall, and it kept them there to support the economic recovery for seven years. The Fed's three rounds of quantitative easing also provided significant fuel for growth, helping the economy weather a series of negative events, including a sovereign debt crisis in Europe, without lapsing back into recession. And its purchases of mortgage-backed securities were crucial to the recovery of the housing market.

Ben's successors at the Federal Reserve, Janet Yellen and Jerome Powell, have begun a gradual process of unwinding the $4.5 trillion book of securities the Fed accumulated through quantitative easing, while slowly nudging interest rates above 2 percent as we write these words. However, it appears that even once monetary policy returns to a neutral stance, the prevailing interest rates will be lower than in the past. If so, the Fed won't have as much headroom to loosen policy with rate cuts if the economy falters, which could hinder efforts to fight a future crisis or recession.

On the fiscal side, the federal deficit at the onset of the last crisis was only about 1 percent of GDP. That increased dramatically once the Great Recession began and tax revenues withered, but the United States still had a fair amount of fiscal capacity to support the economy by expanding deficits in the short term without busting the budget for the long term. And it did. The $150 billion tax cut Hank negotiated early in the crisis, Obama's $800 billion Recovery Act, and the series of smaller follow-up stimulus measures added up to more than 10 percent of GDP. Even though some of this federal stimulus was offset by state and local budget cuts and tax increases, and we believe Washington pivoted too quickly toward fiscal austerity after the recovery began, it's clear that the injection of government adrenaline into the economic bloodstream helped end the recession and launch a gradual recovery, while helping to avert a collapse of the financial system.

After ballooning above $1 trillion during the crisis, the deficit initially fell back to earth as the emergency subsided, the financial rescues were repaid, and the economy rebounded, while Congress raised taxes and cut the rate of growth in spending. But now the annual deficit is soaring above $1 trillion again, because of major tax cuts unaccompanied by spending restraint. As an aging population puts additional strain on future entitlement obligations, the United States could face unsustainable long-term deficits as far as the eye can see. The federal debt held by the public has already risen from 31 percent of GDP in 2001 to 76 percent today, and interest payments alone cost more than $300 billion a year. When the next crisis or even an ordinary downturn hits, depressing tax revenues and making the deficit even worse, policymakers will find it much more difficult, both politically and economically, to match the forceful response of a decade ago. In other words, the use of fiscal adrenaline could be limited just when it is needed most.

It will take a long period of less profligate policy choices and benign economic conditions to restore America's macroeconomic firepower to levels that could help end another emergency. Right now, even a modest recession could leave Washington without much fiscal leeway to respond to a financial crisis, or for that matter to upgrade infrastructure, tackle the opioid epidemic, address climate change, stabilize Social Security, or provide permanent tax relief for hardworking families. America was grappling with rising income inequality, middle-class insecurity, and other economic challenges well before the crisis of 2008, but the crisis made them worse, and unsustainable budget deficits could hobble our ability to deal with them.

The financial system seems stronger today, and in some ways the economy seems more stable as well. Banks are safer and are providing the credit the economy needs to grow. But the world is full of risks. Although the extreme crisis is rare, someday it will come. And even though Washington is mired in a noisy state of gridlock, now is as good a time as any to fill in the gaps in the 2010 reforms and help prepare for the worst. That's the way to make sure the worst doesn't happen. As the Chinese philosopher and military strategist Sun Tzu supposedly warned: If you want peace, prepare for war.

WHAT IS TO BE DONE?

For us, the crisis still feels like yesterday, as it does to many Americans whose lives and livelihoods were disrupted and damaged by those events. But markets have short memories, and as history has demonstrated, long periods of confidence and stability can produce overconfidence and instability. Rules that seem necessary in the aftermath of a disaster start to feel onerous in calmer times.

The enemy is forgetting. The current regulatory burden has not prevented banks from enjoying healthy profits or lending record amounts to households and businesses, but the financial industry is pushing hard for regulatory relief. We believe the first rule for additional financial reform should be Hippocratic: First, do no harm. We should be careful, even as we refine some of the post-crisis reforms, not to allow a general weakening of the most powerful defenses against crisis. When times are good, the dangers of backsliding can seem negligible.

But the costs of the worst financial crises can be so enormous that there ought to be a serious push for even stronger measures both to prevent them and to mitigate them when they occur. It's hard to get the political system to act without a crisis to force its hand, as we learned with our early proposals to fix Fannie Mae and Freddie Mac. In times of calm, politicians are especially reluctant to give central bankers and finance ministries sufficient power to respond to future turbulence, as if the mere existence of a firehouse might cause fires. But it's much safer to give firefighters the firefighting authority they need before the fire starts burning. And the stakes are high enough that Washington ought to treat financial stability as an emergency before it becomes one.

When it comes to crisis prevention, the new capital, leverage, liquidity, and margin rules are much stronger than the safeguards in place before the crisis, and the main challenge for reformers will be to beat back the pressure to weaken them. A related challenge will be that market participants will adapt to the new rules over time, diverting risk to areas where oversight seems looser, so regulators will need the discretion to adapt as well. Commercial banks are still a smaller portion of the U.S. financial system than they are in other major economies, and vigilance will be required to ensure that risky leverage doesn't migrate to new shadows. The next war is unlikely to unfold in exactly the same way as the last one, so it will be vital to make sure regulators have enough flexibility to monitor new dangers as they arise.

The balkanized financial regulatory system could still use reform as well, to reduce turf battles among redundant agencies with overlapping responsibilities. We realize reorganization would be a heavy lift on Capitol Hill, but a more rational regulatory structure could help prevent the Lehmans, AIGs, and WaMus of tomorrow from falling through the regulatory cracks. Otherwise, though, financial fire prevention is in decent shape.

As we've emphasized in this chapter, we're more worried about the ill-equipped financial firehouse. We know the public is not clamoring to make it easier for our successors to rescue banks, but disempowering financial rescuers will not prevent financial rescues. It will only delay them, and make them much costlier.

Somehow, Washington needs to muster the courage to restock the emergency arsenal with the tools that helped end the crisis of 2008—the authority for crisis managers to inject capital into banks, buy their assets, and especially to guarantee their liabilities, the most powerful weapon governments have for quelling panics. The FDIC already has most of these authorities when dealing with commercial banks, and we should be investigating how to extend them to any institution engaged in maturity transformation. The resolution authority in Dodd-Frank also needs to be enhanced, so that when large complicated banks are on the brink of failure, the FDIC can fully stand behind their obligations while winding them down in an orderly fashion. That may create some short-term losses for taxpayers, but the FDIC can recoup those losses from the industry after the crisis passes. By contrast, imposing haircuts on creditors in the midst of a crisis can accelerate a systemic panic and drag down additional firms, which ultimately creates much larger losses for taxpayers. The impulse to ensure that risk takers pay a price for their risk taking is understandable, but requiring crisis managers to extract that price when the crisis is raging only makes it harder to end the crisis.

What makes the FDIC model work so well is that it requires financial firms to pay into an insurance fund prospectively, *before* a crisis strikes—and makes clear that if the price of stabilizing the system turns out to be steeper than anticipated, the industry will eventually foot the bill. We would like to see Congress adopt a similar insurance model that would work for the broader financial system, so crisis managers would have the leeway to put public dollars at risk with the assurance that any shortfalls would ultimately be repaid by financial institutions rather than taxpayers. We're not so naïve as to think this would solve the political problems of financial crisis management. Government efforts to calm financial panics will always be susceptible to attack as unwarranted bailouts for irresponsible speculators. But an up-front legal mandate that the financial industry will pay all the costs of financial firefighting could at least reduce those concerns. We achieved this in practice, in that our approach essentially forced the financial system to pay for the protection we provided, but it would be better if that principle was clear and understood in advance.

Finally, we hope that now that the sun is shining, Washington will use this opportunity to fix its economic roof before the next hard rain. This would begin with a new commitment to fiscal responsibility, because the current dessert-over-vegetables approach of slashing taxes while boosting spending in good times will make it impossible to provide fiscal stimulus in bad times. But we should also be taking steps to address long-standing structural problems, including growing disparities in income that undermine the health of both our economy and our democracy. We need to find ways to have more Americans participate in the nation's economic success. Not only is that the right thing to do, but a stronger economy with more opportunity and prosperity for people from all walks of life will leave the country better prepared to withstand the shocks that economies are heir to, including financial shocks.

Unfortunately, our divided and paralyzed political system

seems incapable of thinking ahead and making tough choices about the future. A decade ago, we did see Democrats and Republicans set aside political and ideological differences to save the country from catastrophe, reinforcing the belief that the United States, when confronted with crisis, and only when confronted with crisis, tends to do what is necessary. But that was hard to do at the time, and it might be harder in a future crisis. We are not naïve about the difficulties of getting it done before the next crisis hits.

Still, the current mix of constraints on the emergency policy arsenal is dangerous for the United States—and, considering the global importance of the U.S. financial system and the dollar, dangerous for the world. We can do better, and the stakes are so huge that doing even a little better could have tremendous benefits in terms of improved well-being. There's no time like the present to start.

ACKNOWLEDGMENTS

MANY PEOPLE HELPED BRING THIS BOOK TO FRUITION. Michael Grunwald provided invaluable help. Scott Moyers, our editor at Penguin, shepherded the project through publication. We thank them both. Thanks are also due to Deborah McClellan for her editorial guidance, to Monica Boyer for fact checking, and to Bob Barnett for legal advice. Andrew Metrick and David Wessel provided valuable insights as we looked back at lessons from the crisis. The charts were the result of a collaboration led by Tim Geithner and Nellie Liang with contributions from Eric Dash, Seth Feaster, Ben Henken, Aidan Lawson, and Deborah McClellan.

CHARTING THE FINANCIAL CRISIS
U.S. Strategy and Outcomes

INTRODUCTION

THE GLOBAL FINANCIAL CRISIS AND GREAT RECESSION OF 2007–2009 constituted the worst shocks to the United States economy in generations. Books have been and will be written about the housing bubble and bust, the financial panic that followed, the economic devastation that resulted, and the steps that various arms of the U.S. and foreign governments took to prevent the Great Depression 2.0. But the story can also be told graphically, as these charts aim to do.

What comes quickly into focus is that as the crisis intensified, so did the government's response. Although the seeds of the harrowing events of 2007–2009 were sown over decades, and the U.S. government was initially slow to act, the combined efforts of the Federal Reserve, Treasury Department, and other agencies were ultimately forceful, flexible, and effective. Federal regulators greatly expanded their crisis management tool kit as the damage unfolded, moving from traditional and domestic measures to actions that were innovative and sometimes even international in reach. As panic spread, so too did their efforts broaden to quell it. In the end, the government was able to stabilize the system, restart key financial markets, and limit the extent of the harm to the economy.

No collection of charts, even as extensive as this, can convey all the complexities and details of the crisis and the government's interventions. But these figures capture the essential features of one of the worst episodes in American economic history and the ultimately successful, even if politically unpopular, government response.

ACRONYMS

ABCP	asset-backed commercial paper
ABS	asset-backed securities
AMLF	Asset-Backed Commercial Paper Money Market Mutual Fund Liquidity Facility
CAP	Capital Assistance Program
CDCI	Community Development Capital Initiative
CDS	credit default swaps
CET1	Common Equity Tier 1
CPFF	Commercial Paper Funding Facility
CPP	Capital Purchase Program
DGP	Debt Guarantee Program
DIF	Deposit Insurance Fund
EESA	Emergency Economic Stabilization Act of 2008
FDIC	Federal Deposit Insurance Corporation
FHA	Federal Housing Administration
FHFA	Federal Housing Finance Agency
GDP	gross domestic product
GSEs	government-sponsored enterprises
HAMP	Home Affordable Modification Program
HARP	Home Affordable Refinance Program
HUD	U.S. Department of Housing and Urban Development
Libor-OIS	London Interbank Offered Rate–Overnight Indexed Swap rate

MBS	mortgage-backed securities
MLEC	Master Liquidity Enhancement Conduit
MMF	money market fund
NBER	National Bureau of Economic Research
PDCF	Primary Dealer Credit Facility
PPIP	Public-Private Investment Program
QE	Quantitative Easing
SAAR	seasonally adjusted annual rate
SBA 7(a)	Small Business Administration 7(a) Securities Purchase Program
SCAP	Supervisory Capital Assessment Program
SDR	special drawing right
SPSPAs	Senior Preferred Stock Purchase Agreements
TAF	Term Auction Facility
TAGP	Transaction Account Guarantee Program
TALF	Term Asset-Backed Securities Loan Facility
TARP	Troubled Assets Relief Program
TLGP	Temporary Liquidity Guarantee Program
TSLF	Term Securities Lending Facility

CHARTING THE FINANCIAL CRISIS

—

U.S. Strategy and Outcomes

Antecedents of the Crisis

In the years leading up to the crisis, the underlying performance of the U.S. economy had eroded in important ways.

Because the growth of productivity and the labor force had slowed in the decade before the crisis, the potential economic growth rate was falling.

Growth in real potential GDP

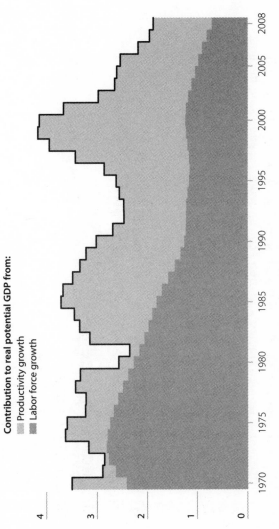

Contribution to real potential GDP from:

Productivity growth
Labor force growth

Sources: Congressional Budget Office, "An Update to the Economic Outlook: 2018 to 2028"; authors' calculations

Overall prime-age participation in the labor force had been falling, as the participation of women slowed and men's continued a decades-long decline.

Civilian labor force participation rates for people ages 25–54, indexed to January 1990=100

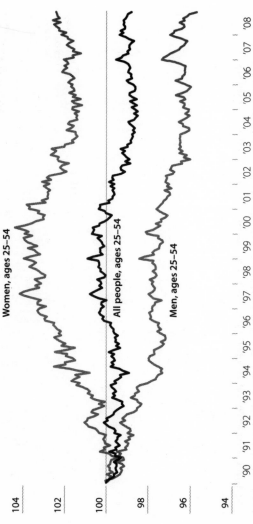

Women, ages 25–54

All people, ages 25–54

Men, ages 25–54

| | | | | | | | | | | | | | | | | | | |
'90 '91 '92 '93 '94 '95 '96 '97 '98 '99 '00 '01 '02 '03 '04 '05 '06 '07 '08

106

104

102

100

98

96

94

Source: Bureau of Labor Statistics via Haver Analytics

Income growth for the top 1 percent had risen sharply, driving income inequality to levels not seen since the 1920s.

Cumulative growth in average income since 1979, before transfers and taxes, by income group

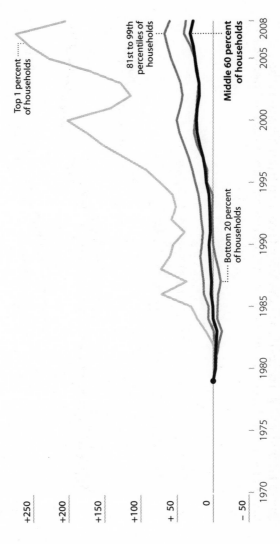

Source: Congressional Budget Office, "The Distribution of Household Income, 2014"

Meanwhile, the financial system was becoming increasingly fragile.

A "quiet period" of relatively low bank losses had extended for nearly 70 years and created a false sense of strength.

Two-year historical loan-loss rates for commercial banks

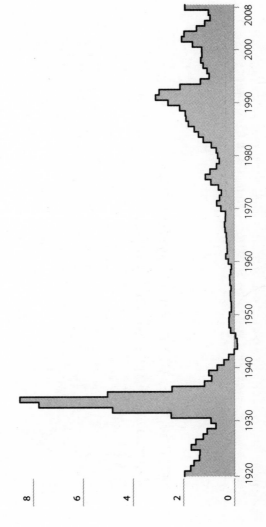

Sources: Federal Deposit Insurance Corp.; Federal Reserve Board; International Monetary Fund

The "Great Moderation"—two decades of more stable economic outcomes with shorter, shallower recessions and lower inflation—had added to complacency.

Quarterly real GDP growth, percent change from preceding period

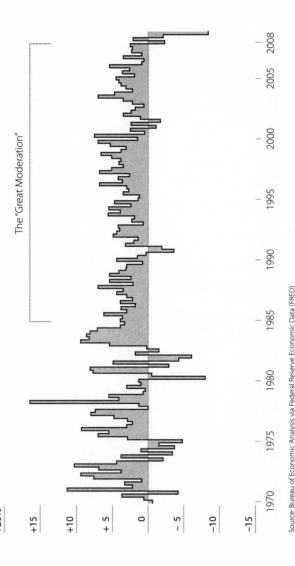

Source: Bureau of Economic Analysis via Federal Reserve Economic Data (FRED)

Long-term interest rates had been falling for decades, reflecting decreasing inflation, an aging workforce, and a rise in global savings.

Benchmark interest rates, monthly

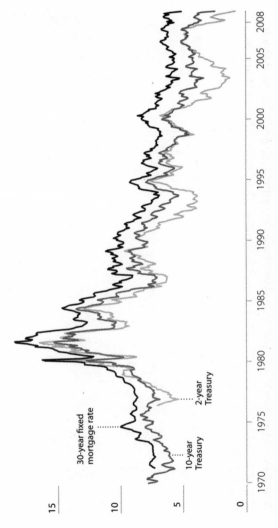

Sources: Federal Reserve Board and Freddie Mac Primary Mortgage Market Survey® via Federal Reserve Economic Data (FRED)

Home prices across the country had been rising rapidly for nearly a decade.

Real home price index, percentage change from 1890

Home prices had increased modestly through several boom-and-bust cycles since the 1970s, but started a much more dramatic rise in the late 1990s.

Source: U.S. Home Price and Related Data, Robert J. Shiller, *Irrational Exuberance*

Household debt as a share of income had risen to alarming heights.

Aggregate household debt as a share of disposable personal income

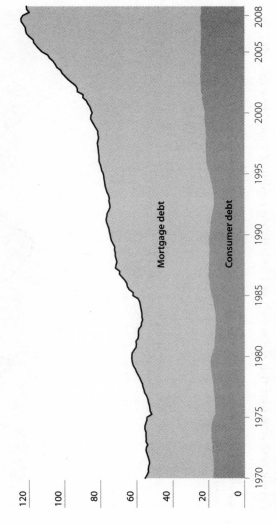

Source: Federal Reserve Board Financial Accounts of the United States, based on Ahn et al. (2018)

Credit and risk had migrated outside the regulated banking system.

Credit market debt outstanding, by holder, as a share of nominal GDP

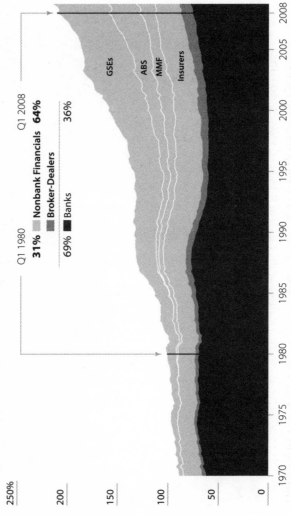

Source: Federal Reserve Board Financial Accounts of the United States   Notes: GSE: government-sponsored enterprise (including Fannie Mae and Freddie Mac);
ABS: asset-backed securities issuers; MMF: money market funds

The amount of financial assets financed with short-term liabilities had also risen sharply, increasing the vulnerability of the financial system to runs.

Net repo funding to banks and broker-dealers

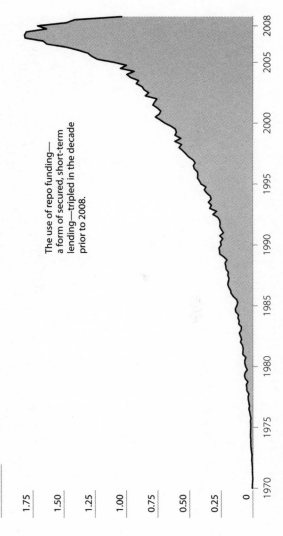

The use of repo funding—
a form of secured, short-term
lending—tripled in the decade
prior to 2008.

Source: Federal Reserve Board Financial Accounts of the United States

The Arc of the Crisis

The financial crisis unfolded in several phases.

Bank credit default swap spreads and Libor-OIS spread

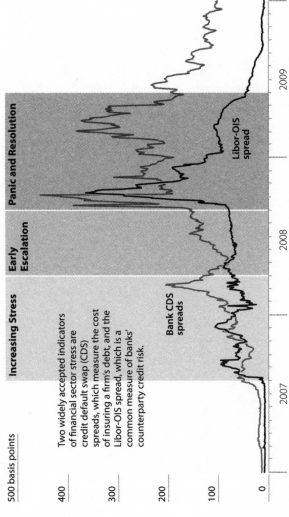

500 basis points

400

Two widely accepted indicators
of financial sector stress are
credit default swap (CDS)
spreads, which measure the cost
of insuring a firm's debt, and the
Libor-OIS spread, which is a
common measure of banks'
counterparty credit risk.

300

200

100

0

2007

Increasing Stress

Early Escalation

Panic and Resolution

2008

2009

Bank CDS spreads

Libor-OIS spread

Sources: Libor-OIS: Bloomberg Finance L.P.; bank CDS spreads: Bloomberg Finance L.P., IHS Markit   Notes: Credit default swap spreads are equal-weighted averages of JPMorgan Chase, Citigroup, Wells Fargo, Bank of America, Morgan Stanley, and Goldman Sachs. Libor-OIS spread used throughout is the spread between the 3-month London Interbank Offered Rate and the 3-month USD overnight indexed swap rate.

ARC OF THE CRISIS

Home prices peaked nationally in the summer of 2006, then fell rapidly—eight major cities had declines of more than 20 percent by March 2008.

Change in S&P CoreLogic Case-Shiller Home Price Indexes for 20 cities and U.S., from U.S. peak in July 2006, not seasonally adjusted

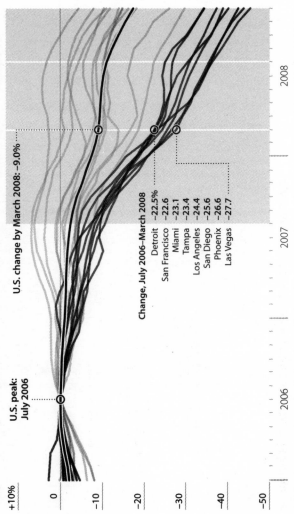

U.S. change by March 2008: −9.0%

U.S. peak: July 2006

Change, July 2006–March 2008

Detroit	−22.5%
San Francisco	−22.6
Miami	−23.1
Tampa	−23.4
Los Angeles	−24.4
San Diego	−25.6
Phoenix	−26.6
Las Vegas	−27.7

+10%

0

−10

−20

−30

−40

−50

2006   2007   2008

Sources: S&P CoreLogic Case-Shiller Home Price Indexes for 20 individual cities and National Home Price Index via Federal Reserve Economic Data (FRED)

Stress in the financial system built up gradually over late 2007 and early 2008, as mortgage troubles and recession fears increased.

Libor-OIS spread

400 basis points

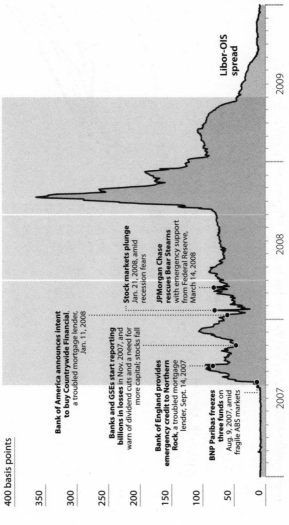

350

300

**Bank of America announces intent
to buy Countrywide Financial,**
a troubled mortgage lender,
Jan. 11, 2008

250

**Banks and GSEs start reporting
billions in losses** in Nov. 2007, and
warn of dividend cuts and a need for
more capital; stocks fall

200

Stock markets plunge
Jan. 21, 2008, amid
recession fears

**Bank of England provides
emergency credit to Northern
Rock,** a troubled mortgage
lender, Sept. 14, 2007

150

**JPMorgan Chase
rescues Bear Stearns**
with emergency support
from Federal Reserve,
March 14, 2008

100

**BNP Paribas freezes
three funds** on
Aug. 9, 2007, amid
fragile ABS markets

50

0

2007   2008   2009

Libor-OIS
spread

Source: Bloomberg Finance L.P.
Note: GSE: government-sponsored enterprise

155

ARC OF THE CRISIS

Investors were fearful that the mortgage giants Fannie Mae and Freddie Mac might collapse and cause severe damage to the housing market.

Stock price of Fannie Mae and Freddie Mac

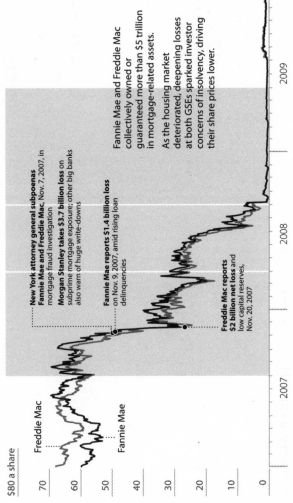

$80 a share

Freddie Mac

Fannie Mae

New York attorney general subpoenas Fannie Mae and Freddie Mac, Nov. 7, 2007, in mortgage fraud investigation

Morgan Stanley takes $3.7 billion loss on subprime mortgage exposure; other big banks also warn of huge write-downs

Fannie Mae reports $1.4 billion loss on Nov. 9, 2007, amid rising loan delinquencies

Freddie Mac reports $2 billion net loss and low capital reserves, Nov. 20, 2007

Fannie Mae and Freddie Mac collectively owned or guaranteed more than $5 trillion in mortgage-related assets.

As the housing market deteriorated, deepening losses at both GSEs sparked investor concerns of insolvency, driving their share prices lower.

2007   2008   2009

Source: The Center for Research in Security Prices at Chicago Booth via Wharton Research Data Services (WRDS)

156

As panic spread, the nation's largest banks and investment banks looked increasingly vulnerable to failure.

S&P 500 Financials index level, and average of six big banks' CDS spreads in basis points

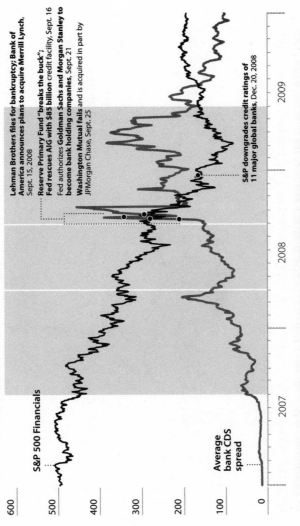

600

500

S&P 500 Financials

400

300

200

Average bank CDS spread

100

0

2007   2008   2009

Lehman Brothers files for bankruptcy; Bank of America announces plans to acquire Merrill Lynch, Sept. 15, 2008

Reserve Primary Fund "breaks the buck"; Fed rescues AIG with $85 billion credit facility, Sept. 16

Fed authorizes Goldman Sachs and Morgan Stanley to become bank holding companies, Sept. 21

Washington Mutual falls and is acquired in part by JPMorgan Chase, Sept. 25

S&P downgrades credit ratings of 11 major global banks, Dec. 20, 2008

Sources: S&P 500 Financials: Bloomberg Finance L.P., S&P Dow Jones Indices LLC; bank CDS spreads: Bloomberg Finance L.P., IHS Markit
Note: Credit default swap spread is an equal-weighted average of JPMorgan Chase, Citigroup, Wells Fargo, Bank of America, Morgan Stanley, and Goldman Sachs.

The rise in losses, the fear of further losses, and the liquidity pressures on the system pushed the price of financial assets down and added to concerns about the solvency of the financial system.

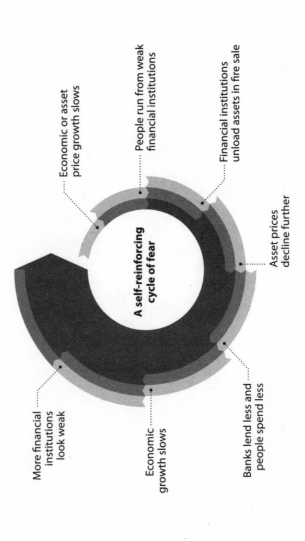

Economic or asset price growth slows

People run from weak financial institutions

Financial institutions unload assets in fire sale

A self-reinforcing cycle of fear

Asset prices decline further

More financial institutions look weak

Economic growth slows

Banks lend less and people spend less

Yet the economic forecasts suggested a modest and manageable slowdown in economic growth. The forecasters were wrong.

Real GDP, percent change from preceding quarter, SAAR, and Philadelphia Fed surveys of professional forecasters

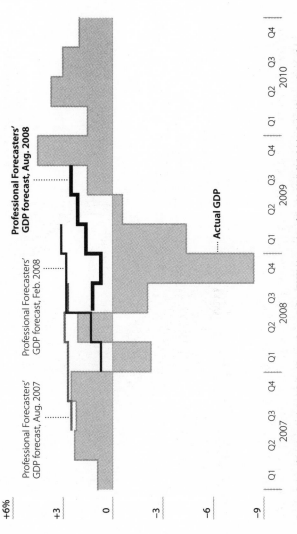

Professional Forecasters'
GDP forecast, Aug. 2007

Professional Forecasters'
GDP forecast, Feb. 2008

**Professional Forecasters'
GDP forecast, Aug. 2008**

Actual GDP

Sources: Bureau of Economic Analysis via Federal Reserve Economic Data (FRED) (data update of Aug. 29, 2018); Philadelphia Federal Reserve Survey of Professional Forecasters, Q3 2007 and Q1 and Q3 2008

The U.S. Strategy

Among the key elements of the U.S. policy response were:

Use of the Fed's lender-of-last-resort authorities beyond the banking system, for investment banks and funding markets.

An expansive use of guarantees to prevent runs on money market funds and a broad array of financial institutions.

An aggressive recapitalization of the financial system, in two stages, backed by expanded FDIC guarantees.

A powerful use of monetary and fiscal policy to limit the severity of the recession and restore economic growth.

A broad mix of housing policies to prevent the failure of the GSEs, slow the fall of home values, lower mortgage rates, and aid in refinancings.

An extension of dollar liquidity to the global financial system, combined with international cooperation and Keynesian stimulus.

U.S. STRATEGY

The U.S. government's initial response to the crisis was gradual, and the tools were limited and antiquated because they were designed for traditional banks.

TOOLS AVAILABLE

FDIC

- Resolution authority for banks, with a systemic risk exception to allow for the provision of broader guarantees

- Deposit insurance for banks

Federal Reserve

- Discount window lending for banks, and in extremis for other institutions

- Swap lines for foreign central banks

NO AUTHORITY

- To intervene to manage the failure of or nationalize nonbanks

- To guarantee the broader liabilities of the financial system

- To inject capital into the financial system

- For the Fed to purchase assets other than Treasuries, Agencies, and Agency MBS*

- To inject capital or guarantee the GSEs

*Agencies are debt securities issued or guaranteed by U.S. federal agencies or GSEs; agency MBS are mortgage-backed securities issued or guaranteed by U.S. federal agencies or GSEs.

162

But the response became more forceful and comprehensive as the crisis intensified and Congress provided new emergency authority.

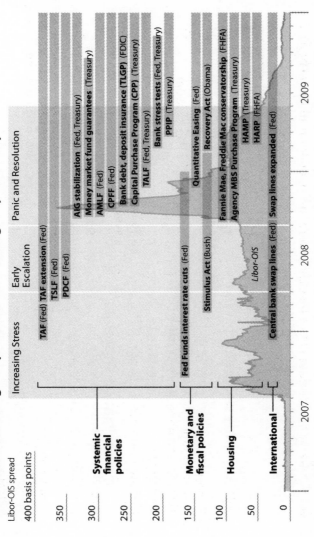

Libor-OIS spread
400 basis points

	Increasing Stress	Early Escalation	Panic and Resolution

Systemic financial policies
- TAF (Fed) TAF extension (Fed)
- TSLF (Fed)
- PDCF (Fed)
- AIG stabilization (Fed, Treasury)
- Money market fund guarantees (Treasury)
- AMLF (Fed)
- CPFF (Fed)
- Bank debt, deposit insurance (TLGP) (FDIC)
- Capital Purchase Program (CPP) (Treasury)
- TALF (Fed, Treasury)
- Bank stress tests (Fed, Treasury)
- PPIP (Treasury)

Monetary and fiscal policies
- Fed Funds interest rate cuts (Fed)
- Stimulus Act (Bush)
- Quantitative Easing (Fed)
- Recovery Act (Obama)

Housing
- Fannie Mae, Freddie Mac conservatorship (FHFA)
- Agency MBS Purchase Program (Treasury)
- HAMP (Treasury)
- HARP (FHFA)

International
- Central bank bank swap lines (Fed) Swap lines expanded (Fed)

Libor-OIS

2007   2008   2009

Source: Libor-OIS; Bloomberg Finance L.P. Note: Start dates for programs reflect the date of their announcement. The Federal Reserve administered the bank stress tests under the SCAP while the Treasury established a capital backstop under the CAP.

The U.S. government deployed a mix of systemic policies to stabilize financial institutions and markets:

Liquidity programs to keep financial institutions operating and credit flowing to consumers and businesses.

Guarantee programs to support critical funding markets for financial institutions.

Capitalization strategies with private and government capital to prevent the failure of systemic institutions and resolve uncertainty about the financial system.

As the crisis intensified, the U.S. government's liquidity programs expanded along several dimensions:

- Domestic $\longrightarrow$ International
- Traditional $\longrightarrow$ Novel
- Institutions $\longrightarrow$ Markets

The Federal Reserve initially deployed its traditional lender-of-last-resort tools to provide liquidity to the banking system.

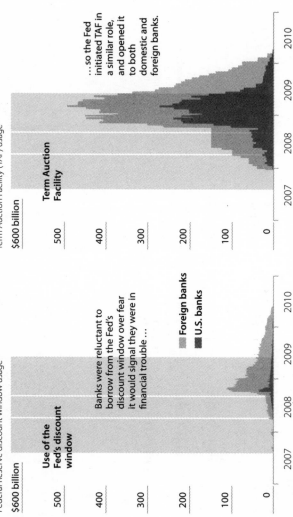

Federal Reserve discount window usage

Term Auction Facility (TAF) usage

$600 billion

$600 billion

Use of the Fed's discount window

Term Auction Facility

Banks were reluctant to borrow from the Fed's discount window over fear it would signal they were in financial trouble ...

...so the Fed initiated TAF in a similar role, and opened it to both domestic and foreign banks.

500
400
300
200
100
0

2007 2008 2009 2010

2007 2008 2009 2010

Foreign banks
U.S. banks

Source: Federal Reserve Board, based on English and Mosser (forthcoming). Transaction-level data on discount window lending during the crisis were released under Freedom of Information Act court decisions (see: https://www.federalreserve.gov/foia/servicecenter.htm)

And then the Fed expanded its tools to support dealers and funding markets.

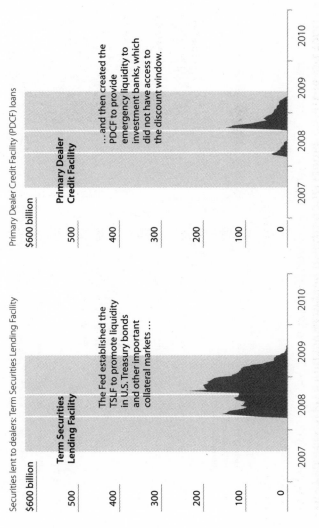

Securities lent to dealers: Term Securities Lending Facility

Primary Dealer Credit Facility (PDCF) loans

Term Securities Lending Facility

The Fed established the TSLF to promote liquidity in U.S. Treasury bonds and other important collateral markets …

Primary Dealer Credit Facility

…and then created the PDCF to provide emergency liquidity to investment banks, which did not have access to the discount window.

Source: Federal Reserve Board via Federal Reserve Economic Data (FRED)
Note: PDCF includes loans extended to select other broker-dealers.

The Fed and Treasury introduced programs to address fragility in the commercial paper market, a key source of funding to financial institutions and businesses.

Overnight issuance as a share of outstanding commercial paper

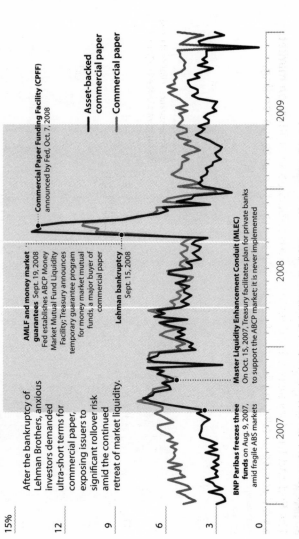

15%

After the bankruptcy of Lehman Brothers, anxious investors demanded ultra-short terms for commercial paper, exposing issuers to significant rollover risk amid the continued retreat of market liquidity.

AMLF and money market guarantees Sept. 19, 2008 Fed establishes ABCP Money Market Mutual Fund Liquidity Facility; Treasury announces temporary guarantee program for money market mutual funds, a major buyer of commercial paper

Commercial Paper Funding Facility (CPFF) announced by Fed, Oct. 7, 2008

Lehman bankruptcy Sept. 15, 2008

BNP Paribas freezes three funds on Aug. 9, 2007, amid fragile ABS markets

Master Liquidity Enhancement Conduit (MLEC) On Oct. 15, 2007, Treasury facilitates plan for private banks to support the ABCP market; it is never implemented

— **Asset-backed commercial paper**
— **Commercial paper**

2007 2008 2009

12
9
6
3
0

Source: Federal Reserve Bank of New York based on data from the Federal Reserve Board of Governors, "Commercial Paper Rates and Outstanding Summary," derived from data supplied by the Depository Trust & Clearing Corporation

The Fed and Treasury also helped restart the asset-backed securitization market, a vital source of funding for credit cards, auto loans, and mortgage lending.

Asset-backed securities issuance (eligible classes) and amount pledged to TALF

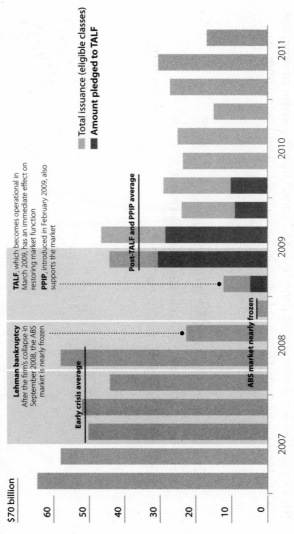

Lehman bankruptcy
After the firm's collapse in September 2008, the ABS market is nearly frozen

TALF, which becomes operational in March 2009, has an immediate effect on restoring market function

PPIP, introduced in February 2009, also supports the market

Early crisis average

ABS market nearly frozen

Post-TALF and PPIP average

Total issuance (eligible classes)
Amount pledged to TALF

$70 billion

60

50

40

30

20

10

0

2007 2008 2009 2010 2011

Sources: Federal Reserve Bank of New York based on data from JP Morgan, Bloomberg Finance L.P., and the Federal Reserve Board of Governors

The U.S. government put in place a mix of guarantees to backstop critical parts of the financial system.

Treasury agreed to guarantee about $3.2 trillion of money market fund assets to stop the run on prime money market funds.

Daily U.S. money market fund flows

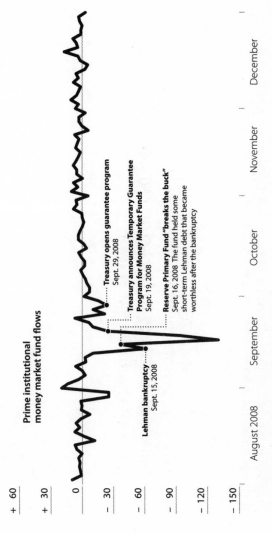

+$ 90 billion

+ 60

+ 30

0

− 30

− 60

− 90

− 120

− 150

Prime institutional money market fund flows

Lehman bankruptcy
Sept. 15, 2008

Reserve Primary Fund "breaks the buck"
Sept. 16, 2008 The fund held some short-term Lehman debt that became worthless after the bankruptcy

Treasury announces Temporary Guarantee Program for Money Market Funds
Sept. 19, 2008

Treasury opens guarantee program
Sept. 29, 2008

August 2008   September   October   November   December

Sources: iMoneyNet; authors' calculations based on Schmidt et al. (2016)

The FDIC expanded its deposit insurance coverage limits on consumer and business accounts in an effort to prevent bank runs.

Share of total deposits FDIC insured

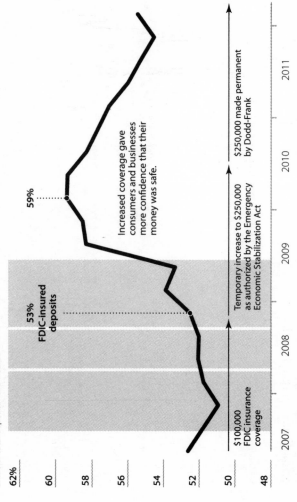

Increased coverage gave consumers and businesses more confidence that their money was safe.

$100,000 FDIC insurance coverage

Temporary increase to $250,000 as authorized by the Emergency Economic Stabilization Act

$250,000 made permanent by Dodd-Frank

53% FDIC-insured deposits

59%

Source: U.S. Treasury, "Reforming Wall Street, Protecting Main Street"
Note: Does not include non-interest-bearing transaction account amounts insured by Dodd-Frank through the end of 2012.

By agreeing to guarantee new financial debt, the FDIC helped institutions obtain more stable funding.

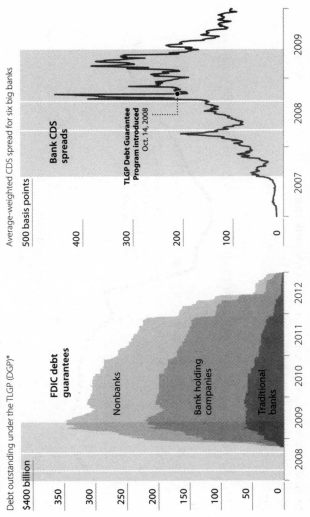

Debt outstanding under the TLGP (DGP)*

$400 billion

- 350
- 300
- 250
- 200
- 150
- 100
- 50
- 0

FDIC debt guarantees

Nonbanks

Bank holding companies

Traditional banks

2008 2009 2010 2011 2012

Average-weighted CDS spread for six big banks

500 basis points

- 400
- 300
- 200
- 100
- 0

Bank CDS spreads

TLGP Debt Guarantee Program introduced
Oct. 14, 2008

2007 2008 2009

Sources: Debt issuance: Federal Deposit Insurance Corp., authors' calculations; CDS spreads: Bloomberg Finance L.P., IHS Markit.
*Debt Guarantee Program covered debt issued by both the parent company and its affiliates.

The U.S. government moved to strengthen the capital in the financial system as the crisis intensified by:

Encouraging the biggest institutions to raise private capital early in the crisis.

Injecting substantial government capital into the banking system when the crisis worsened and Congress provided emergency authority.

Stabilizing the most troubled banks with additional capital and ring-fence guarantees.

Conducting stress tests to complete the recapitalization of the financial system.

As losses worsened early in the crisis, U.S. policymakers urged financial institutions to raise private capital.

Private capital raised between Jan. 1, 2007, and Oct. 13, 2008, for the nine banks receiving initial government investments

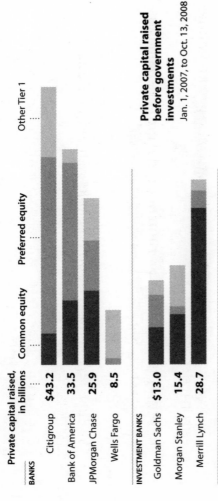

Private capital raised, in billions

Common equity · Preferred equity · Other Tier 1

BANKS

Citigroup $43.2
Bank of America 33.5
JPMorgan Chase 25.9
Wells Fargo 8.5

INVESTMENT BANKS

Goldman Sachs $13.0
Morgan Stanley 15.4
Merrill Lynch 28.7

TRUST AND PROCESSING BANKS

BNY Mellon $0
State Street 4.1

Private capital raised before government investments
Jan. 1, 2007, to Oct. 13, 2008

Source: Goldman Sachs

Then, as panic followed the collapse of Lehman Brothers, Treasury made large capital investments in the biggest banks using new authority from Congress …

Government and other capital raised between Oct. 14, 2008, and May 6, 2009, the day before stress test results were released

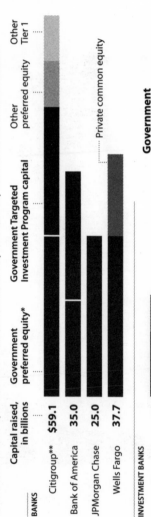
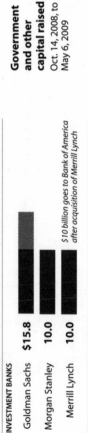

	Capital raised, in billions	Government preferred equity*	Government Targeted Investment Program capital	Other preferred equity	Other Tier 1
BANKS					
Citigroup**	$59.1				
Bank of America	35.0				
JPMorgan Chase	25.0				
Wells Fargo	37.7				

Private common equity

Government and other capital raised
Oct. 14, 2008, to May 6, 2009

INVESTMENT BANKS		
Goldman Sachs	$15.8	
Morgan Stanley	10.0	
Merrill Lynch	10.0	

$10 billion goes to Bank of America after acquisition of Merrill Lynch

TRUST AND PROCESSING BANKS		
BNY Mellon	$3.0	
State Street	2.0	

Source: Goldman Sachs

*Includes capital injections made under the Capital Purchase Program (CPP).

**Citigroup later converted approximately $58 billion of preferred stock and other securities into common equity.

...and used additional funds to make direct government investments in hundreds of smaller banks.

Principal outstanding for government bank capital investments

Distribution of banks participating in the Capital Purchase Program

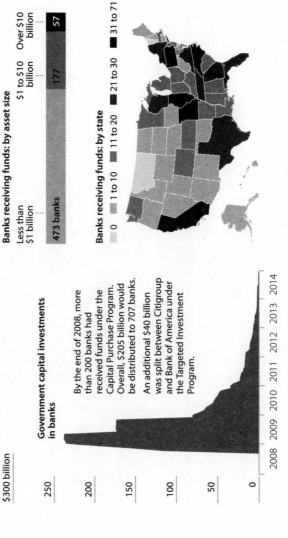

Government capital investments in banks

By the end of 2008, more than 200 banks had received funds under the Capital Purchase Program. Overall, $205 billion would be distributed to 707 banks.

An additional $40 billion was split between Citigroup and Bank of America under the Targeted Investment Program.

Banks receiving funds: by asset size

Less than $1 billion	$1 to $10 billion	Over $10 billion
473 banks	177	57

Banks receiving funds: by state

0   1 to 10   11 to 20   21 to 30   31 to 71

Sources: Timeline of funds outstanding: TARP Tracker; banks receiving funds, by asset size: U.S. Treasury, "Troubled Asset Relief Program: Two Year Retrospective," SNL Financial; banks receiving funds, by state: authors' calculations based on TARP Investment Program transaction reports, Aug. 8, 2018

In addition to capital injections, the government expanded its tools with asset guarantees for the most troubled banks, Citigroup and Bank of America.

Asset Guarantee Program (AGP), Citigroup assets, and "ring-fence" loss responsibility structure
(Asset guarantees for Bank of America were drawn up but never implemented)

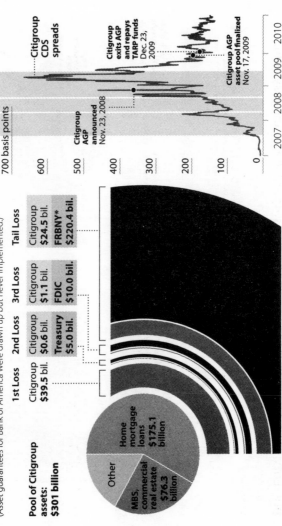

	1st Loss	2nd Loss	3rd Loss	Tail Loss
Pool of Citigroup assets: $301 billion	Citigroup $39.5 bil.	Citigroup $0.6 bil.	Citigroup $1.1 bil.	Citigroup $24.5 bil.
		Treasury $5.0 bil.	FDIC $10.0 bil.	FRBNY* $220.4 bil.

Home mortgage loans $175.1 billion

MBS, commercial real estate $76.3 billion

Other

700 basis points

Citigroup CDS spreads

Citigroup exits AGP and repays TARP funds Dec. 23, 2009

Citigroup AGP announced Nov. 23, 2008

Citigroup AGP asset pool finalized Nov. 17, 2009

600

500

400

300

200

100

0

2007   2008   2009   2010

Sources: Asset Guarantee Program terms: Special Inspector General for TARP, "Extraordinary Financial Assistance Provided to Citigroup, Inc."; CDS spreads: Bloomberg Finance L.P., IHS Markit
*The Federal Reserve Bank of New York's loss position was structured in the form of a nonrecourse loan.

The government provided emergency loans, capital, and guarantees to AIG to prevent a disorderly failure that would have disrupted the financial system.

Outstanding commitment to AIG

In fall of 2010, **AIG spins off AIA** subsidiary in a $20.5 billion IPO and **MetLife acquires ALICO** for $16.2 billion

Recapitalization closes, Jan. 14, 2011: Fed loans are paid off and remaining interests transferred to Treasury which receives 92% of AIG common stock; (Maiden Lane II and III remain with Fed)

Treasury commits $30 billion more; Fed restructures its commitment, including a $25 billion credit facility cut in exchange for preferred stakes in AIG's foreign life insurance subsidiaries AIA and ALICO

$40 billion TARP investment from Treasury; Fed authorizes Maiden Lane II and III to purchase AIG's mortgage-related assets, Nov. 10, 2008

Fed commits additional $37.8 billion Oct. 8, 2008

Fed establishes $85 billion credit facility Sept. 16, 2008, taking a 79.9 percent equity stake in AIG

Government commitments to AIG

Treasury cuts its stake to 77% by selling $5.8 billion in stock, May 2011

Final securities sold from Maiden Lane II Feb. 28, 2012

In a series of stock sales, Treasury cuts its AIG stake to 22% March–Sept. 2012

Government makes $23 billion profit after Treasury sells final shares in AIG, Dec. 2012

Final securities sold from Maiden Lane III Aug. 2012

$200 billion

$150

$100

$50

0

2009   2010   2011   2012

Source: U.S. Treasury   Note: Repayments occurred over the lifetime of the commitment. Any reduction in the commitment, however, is not reflected until the January 2011 recapitalization transaction.

As confidence in banks further eroded, government "stress tests" increased transparency, helping regulators and investors make credible loss projections …

Two-year historical loan-loss rates for commercial banks

SCAP capital shortfall, May 7, 2009

BIGGEST CAPITAL RAISES NEEDED, IN BILLIONS

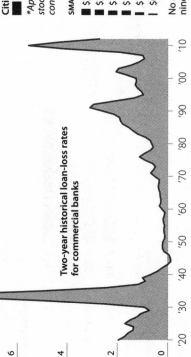

Bank of America $33.9

Wells Fargo $13.7

GMAC $11.5

Citigroup $5.5*

Approximately $58 billion of preferred stock and other securities were later converted into common equity.

SMALLER CAPITAL RAISES NEEDED, IN BILLIONS

$2.5 Regions Financial
$2.2 SunTrust Banks
$1.8 Morgan Stanley
$1.8 KeyCorp
$1.1 Fifth Third Bank
$0.6 PNC Financial

No additional capital was needed at nine other institutions

10%

8

6

4

2

0

9.1%

At 9.1% of outstanding loans, the Fed's loss estimates for the stress test were higher than peak losses during the Great Depression.

Two-year historical loan-loss rates for commercial banks

'20 '30 '40 '50 '60 '70 '80 '90 '00 '10

Sources: Federal Deposit Insurance Corp.; Federal Reserve Board; International Monetary Fund
Note: The 19 largest bank holding companies at the time were subject to the Supervisory Capital Assessment Program (SCAP).

...and accelerated the return of private capital.

Private capital raised, May 7, 2009, through Dec. 31, 2010

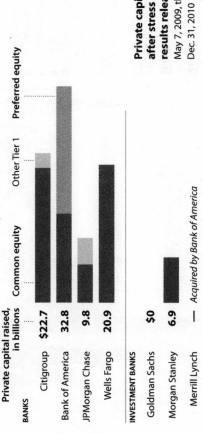

**Private capital raised,
in billions**

BANKS

| | Common equity | Other Tier 1 | Preferred equity |

Citigroup — $22.7
Bank of America — 32.8
JPMorgan Chase — 9.8
Wells Fargo — 20.9

INVESTMENT BANKS

Goldman Sachs — $0
Morgan Stanley — 6.9
Merrill Lynch — *Acquired by Bank of America*

TRUST AND PROCESSING BANKS

BNY Mellon — $2.8
State Street — 2.3

**Private capital raised
after stress test
results released**
May 7, 2009, through
Dec. 31, 2010

Source: Goldman Sachs
Note: In April 2009, before the release of stress test results, Goldman Sachs raised $5.8 billion in capital for the repayment of TARP funds.

U.S. STRATEGY

Indeed, the U.S. recapitalized its banking system more quickly and aggressively than Europe.

Capital raised each year

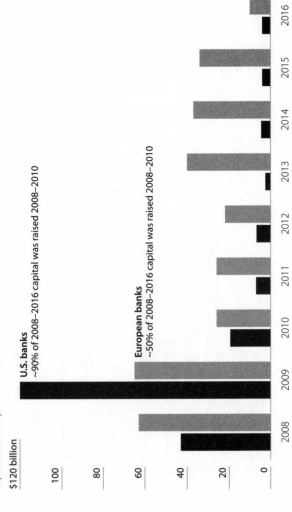

$120 billion

U.S. banks
~90% of 2008–2016 capital was raised 2008–2010

European banks
~50% of 2008–2016 capital was raised 2008–2010

Source: Goldman Sachs
Note: Authors' estimates based on figures from Goldman Sachs.

Alongside programs designed to address the systemic problems in the financial system, the Fed and Treasury put in place a forceful mix of monetary policy and fiscal stimulus.

U.S. STRATEGY

As the Fed funds rate neared zero, the Fed made large-scale asset purchases to drive down long-term interest rates—a policy known as quantitative easing.

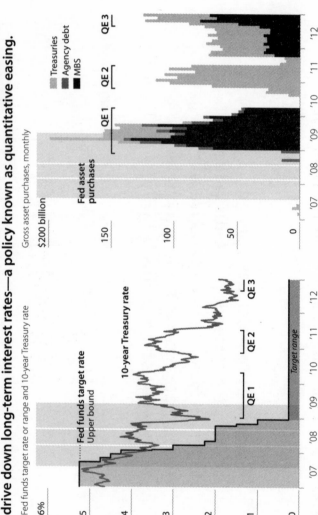

Fed funds target rate or range and 10-year Treasury rate

Gross asset purchases, monthly

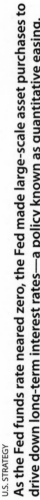

Sources: Target rate: Federal Reserve Board; 10-year Treasury: Federal Reserve Economic Data (FRED); monthly asset purchases: Federal Reserve Bank of New York, Haver Analytics

184

The U.S. passed the first fiscal stimulus very early in the crisis. But at $168 billion, it was relatively small and needed time to take effect.

Quarterly effect of fiscal stimulus measures on GDP

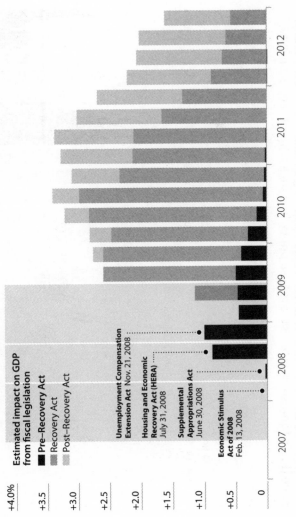

Estimated impact on GDP from fiscal legislation

- Pre–Recovery Act
- Recovery Act
- Post–Recovery Act

Unemployment Compensation Extension Act Nov. 21, 2008

Housing and Economic Recovery Act (HERA) July 31, 2008

Supplemental Appropriations Act June 30, 2008

Economic Stimulus Act of 2008 Feb. 13, 2008

Sources: Council of Economic Advisers; Congressional Budget Office; Bureau of Economic Analysis; calculations by Jason Furman
Note: $168 billion represents the combined stimulus from pre–Recovery Act measures through 2012.

The Recovery Act of 2009 provided a larger mix—$712 billion—of temporary tax cuts and spending increases, offsetting some but not all of the fall in GDP.

Quarterly effect of fiscal stimulus measures on GDP

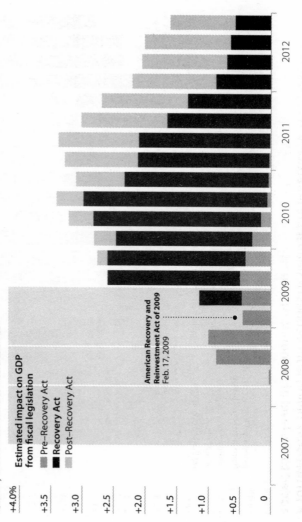

+4.0%

Estimated impact on GDP from fiscal legislation

Pre-Recovery Act
Recovery Act
Post-Recovery Act

+3.5

+3.0

+2.5

+2.0

+1.5

+1.0

+0.5

0

2007   2008   2009   2010   2011   2012

American Recovery and Reinvestment Act of 2009
Feb. 17, 2009

Sources: Council of Economic Advisers; Congressional Budget Office; Bureau of Economic Analysis; calculations by Jason Furman
Note: $712 billion represents the stimulus from the Recovery Act through 2012.

A further $657 billion from a series of smaller post–Recovery Act measures added to the level of economic support ....

Quarterly effect of fiscal stimulus measures on GDP

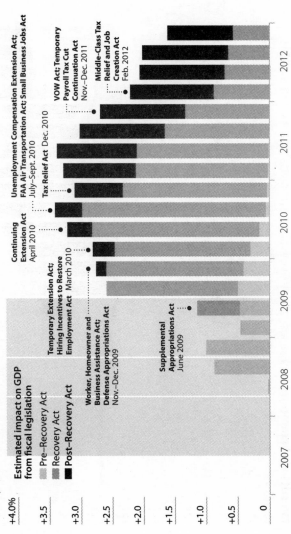

Sources: Council of Economic Advisers; Congressional Budget Office; Bureau of Economic Analysis; calculations by Jason Furman
Note: $657 billion represents the combined stimulus from post–Recovery Act measures through 2012.

... but even as the federal government ramped up stimulus, state and local cutbacks worked against the effort.

Real state and local government purchases during recoveries, 1960–2015, indexed to quarterly level at end of recession

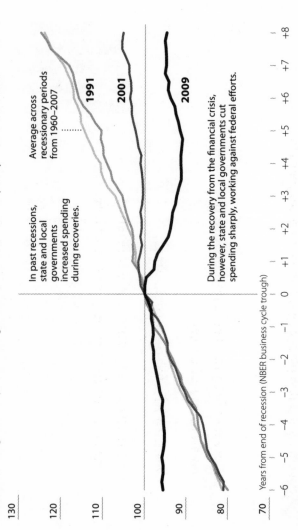

Average across
recessionary periods
from 1960–2007

1991

2001

2009

In past recessions,
state and local
governments
increased spending
during recoveries.

During the recovery from the financial crisis,
however, state and local governments cut
spending sharply, working against federal efforts.

Years from end of recession (NBER business cycle trough)

-6 -5 -4 -3 -2 -1 0 +1 +2 +3 +4 +5 +6 +7 +8

Sources: Bureau of Economic Analysis via Haver Analytics; authors' calculations
Note: Average does not include the 1980 recession owing to overlap with the 1981–82 recession.

The government put in place a series of housing programs to:

- Lower mortgage rates and ensure the availability of credit

- Reduce mortgage foreclosures

- Help struggling borrowers refinance mortgages to take advantage of lower rates

The government's housing programs brought down mortgage rates and reduced foreclosures but were not powerful enough to contain the damage.

30-year fixed mortgage rate

Foreclosure completions, annual rate distributed evenly across four quarters

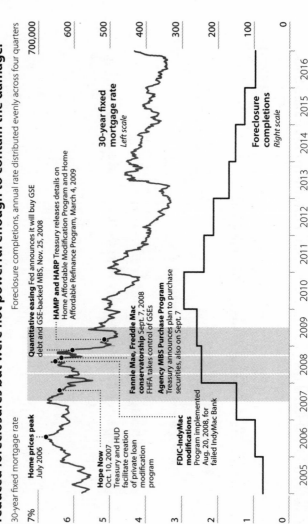

Home prices peak July 2006

Hope Now Oct. 10, 2007 Treasury and HUD facilitate creation of private loan modification program

FDIC-IndyMac modifications Program implemented Aug. 20, 2008, for failed IndyMac Bank

Fannie Mae, Freddie Mac conservatorship Sept. 7, 2008 FHFA takes control of GSEs

Agency MBS Purchase Program Treasury announces plan to purchase securities, also on Sept. 7

Quantitative easing Fed announces it will buy GSE debt and GSE-backed MBS, Nov. 25, 2008

HAMP and HARP Treasury releases details on Home Affordable Modification Program and Home Affordable Refinance Program, March 4, 2009

30-year fixed mortgage rate *Left scale*

Foreclosure completions *Right scale*

Sources: Mortgage rates: Freddie Mac Primary Mortgage Market Survey® via Federal Reserve Economic Data (FRED); foreclosure completions: CoreLogic

U.S. STRATEGY

Government support of Fannie Mae and Freddie Mac kept mortgage credit flowing and stabilized the housing market after private issuers pulled back.

Mortgage-backed securities issuance

Agency MBS to Treasury spread

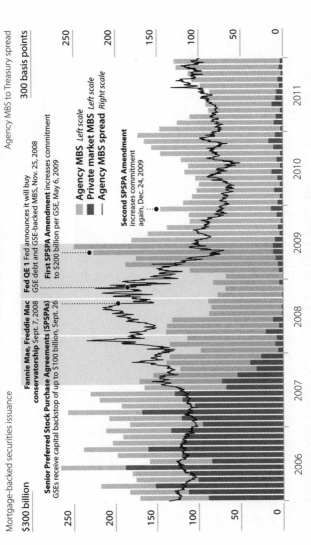

Fannie Mae, Freddie Mac conservatorship Sept. 7, 2008

Senior Preferred Stock Purchase Agreements (SPSPAs) GSEs receive capital backstop of up to $100 billion, Sept. 26

Fed QE 1 Fed announces it will buy GSE debt and GSE-backed MBS, Nov. 25, 2008

First SPSPA Amendment increases commitment to $200 billion per GSE, May 6, 2009

Second SPSPA Amendment increases commitment again, Dec. 24, 2009

Agency MBS *Left scale*

Private market MBS *Left scale*

Agency MBS spread *Right scale*

$300 billion

250

200

150

100

50

0

300 basis points

250

200

150

100

50

0

2006   2007   2008   2009   2010   2011

Sources: MBS Issuance: Securities Industry and Financial Markets Association; agency MBS spread: Bloomberg Finance L.P., authors' calculations

Loan modification programs, including HAMP, helped millions of struggling home owners with their mortgages.

Mortgages modified or receiving loss mitigation aid, April 1, 2009, through Nov. 30, 2016

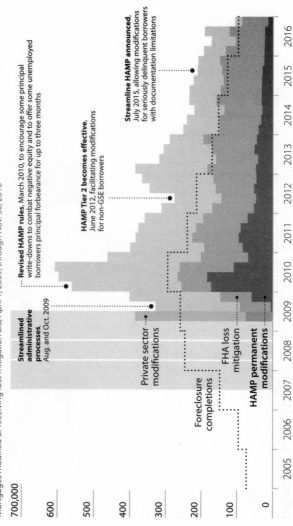

Sources: FHA loss mitigation: Dept. of Housing and Urban Development; HAMP modifications: U.S. Treasury; private sector modifications: HOPE NOW; foreclosure completions: CoreLogic   Note: Modifications through Nov. 2016; other program results through 2016. Foreclosure completions are plotted using an annual rate

The Home Affordable Refinance Program lowered mortgage rates, encouraged refinancings, and helped "underwater" home owners avoid foreclosure.

Loans refinanced through the Home Affordable Refinance Program

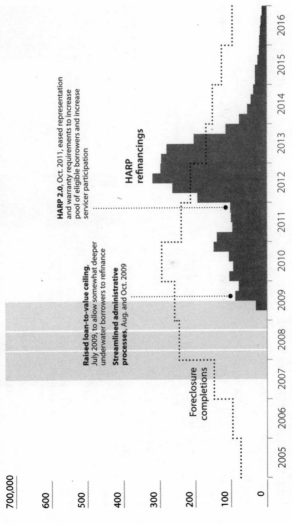

Raised loan-to-value ceiling, July 2009, to allow somewhat deeper underwater borrowers to refinance

Streamlined administrative processes, Aug. and Oct. 2009

HARP 2.0, Oct. 2011, eased representation and warranty requirements to increase pool of eligible borrowers and increase servicer participation

HARP refinancings

Foreclosure completions

Sources: Refinances: Federal Housing Finance Agency; foreclosure completions: CoreLogic
Note: Foreclosure completions are plotted using an annual rate distributed evenly across four quarters.

The government's programs helped millions of home owners, but were slow to take effect and reached a limited number of people threatened by foreclosure.

Home owners assisted through crisis-era loan modification programs and other foreclosure prevention actions

12 million

10

8

6

4

2

0

Special refinancings
9.5 million

PROGRAMS

HARP Completed refinances

FHFA Streamline refinances

FHA Streamline refinances

Through 2017

Through 2012

Loan modifications
8.2 million

PROGRAMS

HAMP All trial and permanent loan modifications

HOPE NOW Proprietary modifications

GSE Standard and streamlined modifications

FHA MODIFICATIONS Additional loss mitigation

Through 2017

Through 2012

Other borrower assistance
5.3 million

PROGRAMS

FHFA HomeSaver advance; repayment plans; forbearance plans; and foreclosure alternatives

FHA Loss mitigation interventions

STATE AND LOCAL HOUSING FINANCE AGENCY INITIATIVES Mortgages and financed units

HARDEST HIT FUND Local foreclosure prevention

Through 2017

Through 2012

Source: Barr et al. (forthcoming)

Even though the crisis started in the United States, its impact reverberated around the world—and the response required U.S. policymakers to work closely with their global counterparts to:

Establish central bank swap lines
to address dollar funding shortages

Coordinate monetary policy
to send a powerful message to the markets

Arrange for IMF support
for emerging markets countries affected by the crisis

U.S. STRATEGY

The Federal Reserve established swap lines with more than a dozen foreign central banks to ease funding pressures arising from a shortage of dollars.

Central bank liquidity swaps

Swap line amounts outstanding

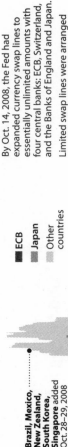

$600 billion

500

400

300

200

100

0

Brazil, Mexico, New Zealand, South Korea, Singapore added Oct. 28–29, 2008

Australia, Denmark, Norway, Sweden added Sept. 24, 2008

Japan, Bank of England, Canada added Sept. 18, 2008

Fed establishes swap lines with the ECB and Switzerland Dec. 12, 2007

2008   2009   2010

ECB

Japan

Other countries

Swap line limits

By Oct. 14, 2008, the Fed had expanded currency swap lines to essentially unlimited amounts with four central banks: ECB, Switzerland, and the Banks of England and Japan.

Limited swap lines were arranged with 10 other central banks:

billions

Canada	$30
Australia	$30
Sweden	$30
Brazil	$30
Mexico	$30
South Korea	$30
Singapore	$30
Denmark	$15
Norway	$15
New Zealand	$15

Sources: Amounts outstanding: Federal Reserve Board, authors' calculations; maximum commitments: Goldberg et al. (2010)

The Federal Reserve and the world's major central banks orchestrated a coordinated interest rate cut.

Central bank target interest rates for each country (month-end)

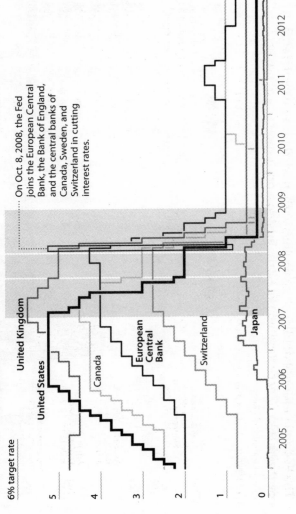

6% target rate

United Kingdom

United States

Canada

European Central Bank

Switzerland

Japan

On Oct. 8, 2008, the Fed joins the European Central Bank, the Bank of England, and the central banks of Canada, Sweden, and Switzerland in cutting interest rates.

Source: Bloomberg Finance L.P.

197

The IMF provided substantial aid to countries affected by the crisis, outpacing its response to the Asian financial crisis in 1997.

Increase in IMF lending commitments from start of Asian and global financial crises

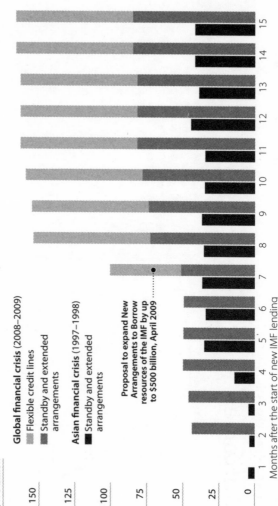

$175 billion

Global financial crisis (2008–2009)
- Flexible credit lines
- Standby and extended arrangements

Asian financial crisis (1997–1998)
- Standby and extended arrangements

Proposal to expand New Arrangements to Borrow resources of the IMF by up to $500 billion, April 2009

Months after the start of new IMF lending

Sources: International Monetary Fund; authors' calculations based on Lowery et al. (forthcoming)   Note: Start date for new IMF lending for the Asian financial crisis (AFC) is July 1997 and for the global financial crisis (GFC) is Sept. 2008. SDR data were converted to U.S. dollars at $1.355820 per SDR (the rate on July 31, 1997) for the AFC and $1.557220 per SDR (the rate on Sept. 30, 2008) for the GFC.

Outcomes

The severity of the stress of the 2008 financial crisis was, in some respects, worse than in the Great Depression.

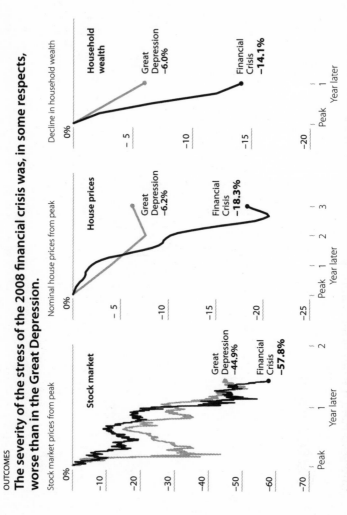

Stock market

Stock market prices from peak

Great Depression **–44.9%**

Financial Crisis **–57.8%**

Peak · Year later · 1 · 2

House prices

Nominal house prices from peak

Great Depression **–6.2%**

Financial Crisis **–18.3%**

Peak · Year later · 1 · 2 · 3

Household wealth

Decline in household wealth

Great Depression **–6.0%**

Financial Crisis **–14.1%**

Peak · Year later · 1

Sources: Stock prices: The Center for Research in Security Prices at Chicago Booth via Wharton Research Data Services (WRDS); housing prices: U.S. home price and related data, Robert J. Shiller, *Irrational Exuberance*; GD household wealth: Mishkin (1978); GR household wealth: Federal Reserve Board Financial Accounts of the United States

The U.S. government response ultimately stopped the panic and stabilized the financial system ...

Bank CDS spreads and Libor-OIS spread

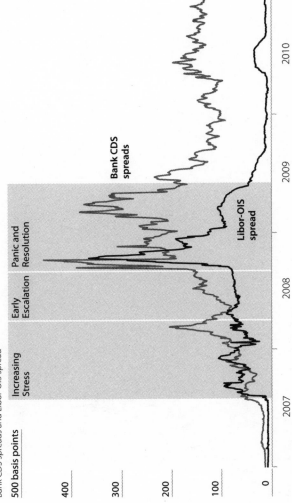

500 basis points

400

300

200

100

0

Increasing Stress

Early Escalation

Panic and Resolution

Bank CDS spreads

Libor-OIS spread

2007

2008

2009

2010

Sources: Libor-OIS: Bloomberg Finance L.P.; CDS spreads: Bloomberg Finance L.P., IHS Markit.
Note: Credit default swap spreads are equal-weighted averages of JPMorgan Chase, Citigroup, Wells Fargo, Bank of America, Morgan Stanley, and Goldman Sachs.

... and allowed the economy to slowly begin digging out of a deep recession.

Treasury, Federal Reserve, and FDIC exposures   Real GDP and employment, year-over-year percent change (monthly)

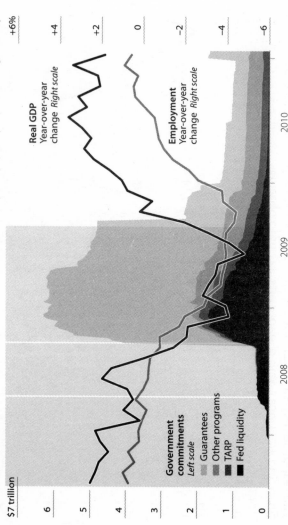

Sources: Liang et al. (forthcoming), based on U.S. government exposures: Congressional Oversight Panel, "Guarantees and Contingent Payments in TARP and Related Programs" via Federal Reserve Bank of St. Louis, Federal Deposit Insurance Corp, Federal Reserve Board, Federal Housing Finance Agency, U.S. Treasury; employment: Bureau of Labor Statistics; real GDP: Macroeconomic Advisers via Haver Analytics

The response helped restart the credit markets and bank lending so that financing was once again cheaper and easier to obtain.

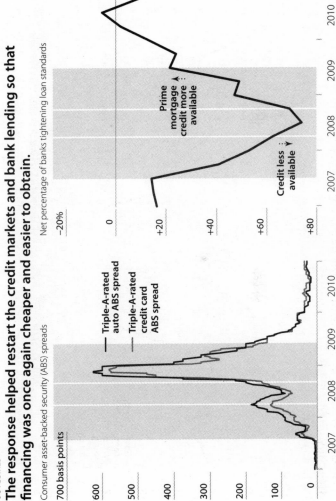

Consumer asset-backed security (ABS) spreads

700 basis points

Triple-A-rated auto ABS spread

Triple-A-rated credit card ABS spread

Net percentage of banks tightening loan standards

−20%

Prime mortgage credit more available

Credit less available

Sources: ABS spreads: Federal Reserve Bank of New York based on data from JP Morgan and Bloomberg Finance L.P.; lending standards: Federal Reserve Board

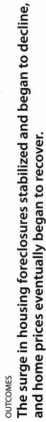

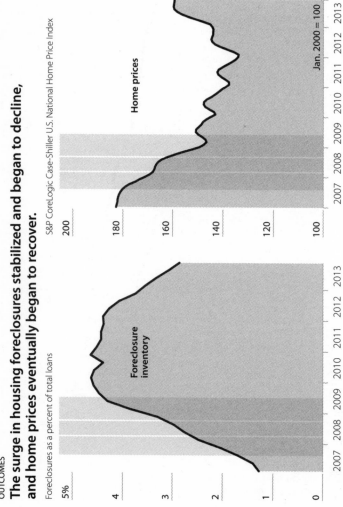

The surge in housing foreclosures stabilized and began to decline, and home prices eventually began to recover.

Foreclosures as a percent of total loans

S&P CoreLogic Case-Shiller U.S. National Home Price Index

5%

4

3

2

1

0

2007 2008 2009 2010 2011 2012 2013

Foreclosure inventory

200

180

160

140

120

100

Home prices

2007 2008 2009 2010 2011 2012 2013

Jan. 2000 = 100

Sources: Foreclosure inventory: Mortgage Bankers Association's National Delinquency Survey, Bloomberg Finance L.P.; home price index: S&P CoreLogic Case-Shiller U.S. National Home Price Index, not seasonally adjusted, via Federal Reserve Economic Data (FRED)

OUTCOMES

The pace of the recovery in the U.S. was slow, as is typical following a severe financial crisis ...

Percentage change in real GDP from peak

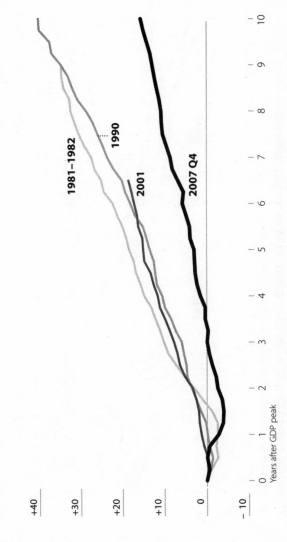

1981–1982

1990

2001

2007 Q4

Years after GDP peak

Source: Bureau of Economic Analysis via Federal Reserve Economic Data (FRED)

205

...although growth has been stronger than in many European countries.

Real GDP, percentage change from 4th quarter 2007

Source: Organisation for Economic Co-operation and Development

Financial crises are typically costly to economic output, but the U.S. strategy was able to limit the damage compared to other crises.

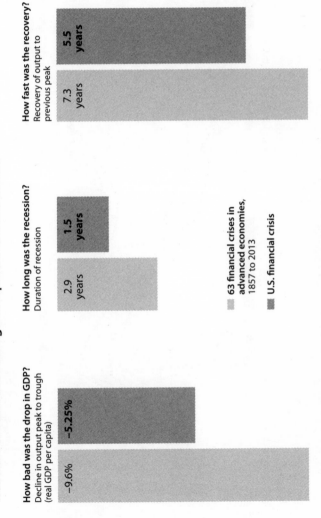

How bad was the drop in GDP?
Decline in output peak to trough
(real GDP per capita)

−9.6%

−5.25%

How long was the recession?
Duration of recession

2.9 years

1.5 years

How fast was the recovery?
Recovery of output to previous peak

7.3 years

5.5 years

63 financial crises in advanced economies, 1857 to 2013

U.S. financial crisis

Sources: Reinhart and Rogoff (2009); Bureau of Economic Analysis via Federal Reserve Economic Data (FRED); based on comparisons from Liang et al. (forthcoming)

207

U.S. taxpayers made a profit on the financial rescue.

Income or cost of financial stability programs

Capital Investments — In billions

	In billions
GSEs	+$88.2
AIG	22.7
CPP	21.9
Citigroup	6.6
Bank of America	3.1
GMAC/Ally	2.4
CDCI	0.0
Chrysler Financial	0.0
Chrysler	–1.2
General Motors	–10.5

Liquidity/ Credit Markets — In billions

	In billions
GSE Debt Purchases	+$17.6
CPFF	6.1
TAF	4.1
PPIP	3.9
TALF	2.3
TSLF	0.8
Maiden Lane	0.8
PDCF	0.6
AMLF	0.5
SBA 7(a)	0.0

FDIC Resolution — In billions

	In billions
Cumulative Income, 2008–10	+$45.4
DIF Losses, 2008–10	–60.0

Guarantee Programs — In billions

	In billions
DGP	+$10.2
MMF Guarantee	1.2
TAGP	–0.3

Sources: Federal Deposit Insurance Corp.; Federal Housing Finance Agency; Federal Reserve Board; Labonte and Webel (2018); U.S. Treasury

Today the financial system has significantly more capital and would be better able to withstand losses in the event of a severe economic downturn.

CET1 and Tier 1 common equity as percent of risk-weighted assets

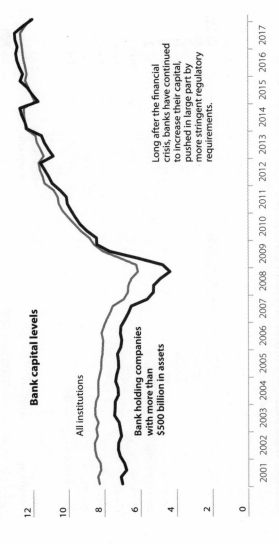

Bank capital levels

All institutions

Bank holding companies
with more than
$500 billion in assets

Long after the financial
crisis, banks have continued
to increase their capital,
pushed in large part by
more stringent regulatory
requirements.

Source: Federal Reserve Bank of New York's Research and Statistics Group
Note: Capital ratio is based on tier 1 common equity pre-2014 and common equity tier 1 (CET1) as of 2015, and is a combination of the two during 2014.

Stronger regulations on capital are applied to a much broader share of the U.S. financial system.

Q4 2007

41% of the financial system faced leverage restrictions

No leverage restrictions

$13.0 trillion Depository Institutions

$7.6 trillion Government-Sponsored Enterprises

$4.6 trillion Asset-Backed Securities

$4.7 trillion Broker-Dealers

$2.1 tn Finance Cos.

$32.1 trillion total financial assets

Q4 2017

92% of the financial system faced leverage restrictions

GSEs remain under government conservatorship

$18.8 trillion Depository Institutions

$8.9 trillion Government-Sponsored Enterprises

$3.2 trillion Broker-Dealers

$1.5 tn Fin. Cos.

$1.2 tn ABS

$33.6 trillion total financial assets

Source: Federal Reserve Board Financial Accounts of the United States

Nonetheless, the emergency authorities available in the U.S. are still too limited to allow an effective response to a severe crisis.

PRE-CRISIS LIMITATIONS

- Limited reach of prudential limits on leverage
- Limited deposit insurance coverage
- No resolution authority for largest bank holding companies and nonbanks
- No ability to inject capital into financial firms
- No authority to stabilize GSEs

ESSENTIAL CRISIS AUTHORITIES

- Fed expanded lender of last resort
- Broader FDIC debt and money market fund guarantees
- GSE conservatorship
- Capital injections into financial firms

POST-CRISIS TOOLS

- Stronger capital requirements
- Stronger liquidity and funding requirements
- Living wills, bankruptcy, and resolution authority

POST-CRISIS LIMITATIONS

- Limitations on Fed lender of last resort
- No money market fund guarantees or FDIC debt guarantees without congressional action
- No authority to inject capital

This was a terribly damaging crisis. It did not need to be so bad.

The damage illustrates the costs of running a financial system with weak oversight, and of going into a crisis without the essential tools for aggressive early action to prevent disaster.

The recovery was slow and fragile, made slower by the premature shift to tighter fiscal policy.

Even after repairing the immediate damage, the U.S. economy still faces a number of longer-term challenges, with causes that predated the crisis.

ACKNOWLEDGMENTS

This chart book was produced as part of an effort led by Ben S. Bernanke, Timothy F. Geithner, and Henry M. Paulson, Jr., to examine the U.S. government's interventions in the 2007–2009 financial crisis, a joint project of the Yale School of Management, Program on Financial Stability, and the Brookings Institution, Hutchins Center on Fiscal and Monetary Policy.

CHART BOOK PROJECT ADVISERS: Timothy F. Geithner and Nellie Liang

EDITORIAL DIRECTOR: Deborah McClellan

CHART BOOK PROJECT DIRECTOR: Eric Dash

DATA VISUALIZATION: Seth W. Feaster

LEAD DATA ANALYST: Ben Henken   **DATA ANALYST:** Aidan Lawson

We wish to thank the following individuals and organizations:

BROOKINGS/HUTCHINS: David Wessel, Director; Sage Belz, Jeffrey Cheng, Vivien Lee, Michael Ng

YALE PROGRAM ON FINANCIAL STABILITY: Andrew Metrick, Program Director; Alec Buchholtz, Anshu Chen, Greg Feldberg, Christian McNamara, Chase Ross, David Tam, Daniel Thompson, Rosalind Z. Wiggins

GOLDEN TRIANGLE STRATEGIES: Monica Boyer, Emily Cincebeaux, Bill Marsh, Melissa Wohlgemuth

OTHERS: Charlie Anderson, Matthew Anderson, Christie Baer, Michael S. Barr, James Egelhof, Jason Furman, Robert Jackson,

Annabel Jouard, Katherine Korsak, Lorie Logan, Francis Mahoney, Vivek Manjunath, Drew McKinley, Patrick Parkinson, Wilson Powell III, Ernie Tedeschi

DATA SOURCES: Bloomberg Finance L. P.; the Center for Research in Security Prices at Chicago Booth; CoreLogic®, a property data and analytics company; Freddie Mac; Goldman Sachs; Haver Analytics; IHS Markit; iMoneyNet; Mortgage Bankers Association; Securities Industry and Financial Markets Association; SNL Financial; S&P Dow Jones Indices LLC, Standard & Poor's (S&P® and S&P 500® are registered trademarks of Standard & Poor's Financial Services LLC, and Dow Jones® is a registered trademark of Dow Jones Trademark Holdings LLC. © 2017 S&P Dow Jones Indices LLC, its affiliates and/or its licensors. All rights reserved); U.S. Dept. of Housing and Urban Development; Wharton Research Data Services (WRDS)

ADDITIONAL DATA SOURCES

Bureau of Economic Analysis; Bureau of Labor Statistics; Congressional Budget Office; Congressional Oversight Panel; Council of Economic Advisers; Federal Deposit Insurance Corp.; Federal Housing Finance Agency; Federal Reserve Bank of New York Financial Crisis Policy Response Timeline; Federal Reserve Bank of New York's Research and Statistics Group; Federal Reserve Bank of Philadelphia; Federal Reserve Bank of St. Louis; Federal Reserve Bank of St. Louis Financial Crisis Policy Response Timeline; Federal Reserve Board; Federal Reserve Economic Data (FRED); International Monetary Fund; Macroeconomic Advisers®; Mishkin (1978); Organisation for Economic Co-operation and Development; U.S. Dept. of Treasury

NOTES

PAGE 143: Re-created with data underlying Figure 10, "The Distribution of Household Income, 2014," Congressional Budget Office (2018), www.cbo.gov/publication/53597. See link for definitions of income and income groups.

PAGE 148: Based on Figure 3.1, U.S. home price and related data, Robert J. Shiller, *Irrational Exuberance*, 3rd ed. (Princeton, NJ: Princeton University Press, 2015), as updated by the author, www.econ.yale.edu/~shiller/data.htm.

PAGE 149: Based on Figure 1, Panel 1, Michael Ahn, Michael Batty, and Ralf Meisenzahl, "Household Debt-to-Income Ratios in the Enhanced Financial Accounts," *FEDS Notes* (Washington, DC: Board of Governors of the Federal Reserve System, January 11, 2018), https://doi.org/10.17016/2380-7172.2138.

PAGE 150: Based on Figure 1, Scott G. Alvarez, William Dudley, and Nellie Liang, "Nonbank Financial Institutions: New Vulnerabilities and Old Tools," in Ben S. Bernanke, Timothy F. Geithner, and Henry M. Paulson, Jr., with Nellie Liang, eds., *First Responders: Inside the U.S. Strategy for Fighting the 2007–2009 Global Financial Crisis* (New Haven: Yale University Press, forthcoming).

PAGE 151: Based on Exhibit 1, Gary Gorton and Andrew Metrick, "Who Ran on Repo?" (2012), http://faculty.som.yale.edu/garygorton/documents/whorancompleteoctober4.pdf.
Banks' portion includes net liabilities from federal funds agreements.

PAGE 166: Based on figures 5 and 6, William English and Patricia Mosser, "The Use and Effectiveness of Conventional Liquidity Tools Early in the Financial Crisis," in Ben S. Bernanke, Timothy F. Geithner, and Henry M. Paulson, Jr., with Nellie Liang, eds. *First Responders: Inside the U.S. Strategy for Fighting the 2007–2009 Global Financial Crisis,* (New Haven: Yale University Press, forthcoming).

PAGE 168: Based on Figure 7, Lorie Logan, William Nelson, and Patrick Parkinson, "The Fed's Novel Lender of Last Resort Programs," in Ben S. Bernanke, Timothy F. Geithner, and Henry M. Paulson, Jr., with Nellie Liang, eds., *First Responders: Inside the U.S. Strategy for Fighting the 2007–2009 Global Financial Crisis* (New Haven: Yale University Press, forthcoming).

PAGE 169: Based on Chart 5, Adam Ashcraft, Allan Malz, and Zoltan Pozsar, "The Federal Reserve's Term Asset-Backed Securities Loan Facility," *Federal Reserve Bank of New York Economic Policy Review* 18(3) (November 2012): 29-66, https://www.newyorkfed.org/medialibrary/media/research/epr/2012/EPRvol18n3.pdf.

PAGE 171: Based on Panel A, Lawrence Schmidt, Allan Timmermann, and Russ Wermers, "Runs on Money Market Mutual Funds," *American Economic Review* 106(9) (2016): 2625–57, www.aeaweb.org/articles?id=10.1257/aer.20140678.

PAGE 172: Based on Slide 4, "Reforming Wall Street, Protecting Main Street," U.S. Treasury, July 2012, www.treasury.gov/connect/blog/Documents/20120719_DFA_FINAL5.pdf.

PAGE 173: Traditional banks include depository institutions. Bank holding companies include bank holding companies, savings and loan holding companies, financial holding companies, and their funding affiliates. Nonbanks include nonbank entities and their affiliates, as well as bank holding companies with nonbank assets of nonbank subsidiaries comprising more than half of their total assets.

PAGE 179: Based on U.S. Treasury data and AIG infographic and timeline, www.treasury.gov/initiatives/financial-stability/TARP-Programs/aig/Pages/default.aspx.

PAGES 185, 186, 187: Based on Figure 3, Jason Furman, "The Fiscal Response to the Great Recession: Steps Taken, Paths Rejected, and Lessons for Next Time," in Ben S. Bernanke, Timothy F. Geithner, and Henry M. Paulson, Jr., with Nellie Liang, eds., *First Responders: Inside the U.S. Strategy for Fighting the 2007–2009 Global Financial Crisis* (New Haven: Yale University Press, forthcoming).

PAGE 191: Monthly mortgage-related securities issuance figures may not match annual figures reported by the Securities Industry and Financial Markets Association on its website owing to a methodological difference in the reporting of each series.

PAGE 192: Based on the figure "Mortgage Aid Extended More than 9.9 Million Times, Outpacing Foreclosures," December 2016 Housing Scorecard, www.hud.gov/sites/documents/SCORECARD_2016_12_508C.PDF.

PAGE 194: Some home owners may have participated in more than one program; the sum of home owners helped across all categories does not necessarily reflect the number of unique borrowers helped.

Based on Table 3, Michael Barr, Neel Kashkari, Andreas Lehnert, Phillip Swagel, "Crisis-Era Housing Programs," in Ben S. Bernanke, Timothy F. Geithner, and Henry M. Paulson, Jr., with Nellie Liang, eds., *First Responders: Inside the U.S. Strategy for Fighting the 2007–2009 Global Financial Crisis* (New Haven: Yale University Press, forthcoming).

PAGE 196: Maximum commitments were taken from Table 2, Linda S. Goldberg, Craig Kennedy, and Jason Miu, "Central Bank Dollar Swap Lines and Overseas Dollar Funding Costs," *Federal Reserve Bank of New York Economic Policy Review* 17(1) (May 2011): 3–20, www.newyorkfed.org/medialibrary/media/research/epr/11v17n1/1105gold.pdf.

PAGE 198: Based on Clay Lowery, Nathan Sheets, and Edwin (Ted) Truman, "International Coordination of Financial and Economic Policies," in Ben S. Bernanke, Timothy F. Geithner, and Henry M. Paulson, Jr., with Nellie Liang, eds., *First Responders: Inside the U.S. Strategy for Fighting the 2007–2009 Global Financial Crisis* (New Haven: Yale University Press, forthcoming).

PAGE 200: The stock market (NYSE/AMEX/NASDAQ/ARCA) is measured by total market value as reported by the Center for Research in Security Prices and is shown to financial crisis trough. House prices are shown to three years after peak. Household wealth is a comparison between the change in the annual average (in nominal terms) of household wealth from 1929 to 1930, and the change in the nominal level of household wealth from Q1 2008 to Q1 2009.

Estimates of real household net worth (wealth) during the Great Depression were taken from Table 1, Frederic S. Mishkin, "The Household Balance Sheet and the Great Depression," *The Journal of Economic History* 38(4) (December 1978): 918–37, www.jstor.org/stable/2118664.

PAGE 202: Guarantees: Reflects the U.S. Treasury's maximum commitments under the Temporary Guarantee Program for Money Market Funds and the FDIC's maximum commitments under the two components of the Temporary Liquidity Guarantee Program, the Debt Guarantee Program and the Transaction Account Guarantee Program.

Troubled Assets Relief Program (TARP): Reflects principal outstanding for TARP programs including bank support programs, credit market programs, auto industry support, assistance to American International Group, and housing programs.

Federal Reserve Liquidity Programs: Reflects loan amounts outstanding under credit and liquidity programs established by the Federal Reserve Board. These include discount window lending (primary credit, secondary credit, and seasonal credit), term auction credit, the Primary Dealer Credit Facility, the Asset-Backed Commercial Paper Money Market Mutual Fund Liquidity Facility, the Term Asset-Backed Securities Loan Facility, the Commercial Paper Funding Facility, and central bank liquidity swaps. Also reflects the value of outstanding securities lent through the Term Securities Lending Facility.

Other Programs: Reflects the Federal Reserve, FDIC, and Treasury's commitments under the Asset Guarantee Program; Federal Reserve Board assistance to Maiden Lane companies and support to American International Group; Treasury support for Fannie Mae and Freddie Mac through the senior preferred stock purchase agreements, as well as the face value of Treasury's total mortgage-backed securities (MBS) portfolio at the end of each month, from October 2008 to March 2012.

Exposures via Treasury's Temporary Guarantee Program for Money Market Funds were taken from "Guarantees and Contingent Payments in TARP and Related Programs: Congressional Oversight Panel November Oversight Report," Congressional Oversight Panel (November 2009), https://fraser.stlouisfed.org/title/5018.

Based on Nellie Liang, Margaret M. McConnell, and Phillip Swagel, "Evidence on Outcomes," in Ben S. Bernanke, Timothy F. Geithner, and Henry M. Paulson, Jr., with Nellie Liang, eds., *First Responders: Inside the U.S. Strategy for Fighting the 2007–2009 Global Financial Crisis* (New Haven: Yale University Press, forthcoming).

PAGE 207: Data for 63 financial crises in advanced economies, 1857 to 2013, were taken from Carmen Reinhart and Kenneth Rogoff, "Recovery from Financial

Crises: Evidence from 100 Episodes," *American Economic Review: Papers & Proceedings* 104(5) (2014): 50–55, https://scholar.harvard.edu/files/rogoff/files/aer_104-5_50-55.pdf.

Based on Nellie Liang, Margaret M. McConnell, and Phillip Swagel, "Evidence on Outcomes," in Ben S. Bernanke, Timothy F. Geithner, and Henry M. Paulson, Jr., with Nellie Liang, eds., *First Responders: Inside the U.S. Strategy for Fighting the 2007–2009 Global Financial Crisis* (New Haven: Yale University Press, forthcoming).

PAGE 208: Based on Table 2 in Baird Webel and Marc Labonte, "Costs of Government Interventions in Response to the Financial Crisis: A Retrospective," Congressional Research Service (updated September 2018), https://fas.org/sgp/crs/misc/R43413.pdf.

All figures except otherwise noted are reported on a cash basis and as of Aug. 1, 2018. GSE debt purchases, DIF losses and cumulative income, and TAGP are as of Dec. 31, 2017; Maiden Lane is as of Jan. 31, 2018; and GSEs are as of 2018 Q2.

PAGE 210: Depository institutions include U.S.-chartered depository institutions, foreign banking offices in the U.S., and credit unions.

Index

Note: Page numbers in *italics* refer to charts and tables in "Charting the Financial Crisis" at the back of the book.

Index

Index

Index

Index

Index

Index

Index

FIREFIGHTING

Ben S. Bernanke, currently a distinguished senior fellow at the Brookings Institution and president of the American Economic Association, was chairman of the Federal Reserve from 2006 to 2014. He is the author of *The Courage to Act: A Memoir of a Crisis and Its Aftermath*.

Timothy F. Geithner is president of Warburg Pincus and was from 2009 to 2013 the seventy-fifth secretary of the Treasury for President Barack Obama's first term. Formerly president of the Federal Reserve Bank of New York, he is the author of *Stress Test: Reflections on Financial Crises*.

Henry M. Paulson, Jr., is founder and chairman of the Paulson Institute and served from 2006 to 2009 as the seventy-fourth secretary of the Treasury under President George W. Bush. Formerly chairman and CEO of Goldman Sachs, he is the author of *On the Brink: Inside the Race to Stop the Collapse of the Global Financial System* and *Dealing with China: An Insider Unmasks the New Economic Superpower*.